Here are some things that people are saying about
Driving with the Light:

"Donna Krueger is a delight! I have known her for years, and I can't
think of a single time I have ever seen her when she did not have a
smile on her face and a word of encouragement for everyone she en-
countered. Donna is a woman of faith who is a joy to be around. She
is someone you would love to go on a journey with. And in her
book, *Driving With The Light*, you will do exactly that. As you read,
you will go on a road trip that will help you see that you will get
through whatever you're facing, and even more, you can come out
stronger than you ever imagined on the other side."

Robert Hotchkin
Author, Speaker, Minister, Media Host
Robert-Hotchkin.com / MenontheFrontlines.com

"The telling of a quest and the unveiling of its experiences and emotions has been one of the most widely used elements in literature from
the earliest recorded manuscripts until now. There is a reason for this;
the human experience is a journey. We are all involved and invested
in self-discovery—a drive to find meaning in hardships and a desire
for communion with God in our everyday encounters. Donna's telling
of her adventurous road trip following widowhood and the paralleling
of her spiritual journey beautifully unveils the depth of God's love for
us all."

Wendy K. Walters
Author, Consultant, Motivational Speaker

Life is difficult. Many people deal with its difficulties by complaining their way through a joyless and directionless existence. Donna Krueger chose a different way. She chose to look to God in the midst of her troubles. Through the tragic death of her husband, the joy and tears of parenting, and the many losses and misfortunes that are a part of life lived in a broken world, Donna bravely chose to turn her face toward the Light. *Driving With The Light* is an account of her late-in-life nine-month RV road trip through which she shares the hard-earned truths and lessons she has learned. As you read this book, you'll be blessed as you travel her journey with her. I have no doubt you will find signs along the way that will help you discover the right roads for your own journey.

Danny Mullins
At His Feet Ministries
Spiritual Director, Sustainable Faith School of Spiritual Direction

Donna Krueger brings us inspiration, courage, and hope as she takes us along on her spiritual journey and motor home road trip across the United States. Your heart will be stirred as she overcomes her personal trials and humbly shares her spiritual growth. I believe many will be brought into a more intimate relationship with God as they read and share her book. Donna is an encouragement and reminder to all of us that it's never too late to step out and follow your dreams!

Chelley Antonczak,
President and CEO of Chelley & Company Ministries
Featured Speaker and Coach
www.chelleyandcompanyministries.com
www.coachchel.com

Having known Donna for more almost three decades, I have anticipated the release of her book. She told me she was writing a book based on her life in comparison with her major RV trip across the country. I was intrigued by the idea. When I finally had a chance to read the book, I was thoroughly blessed by her story and the way she connected it with her spiritual life. The book is humorous and expressive and has deep insights into life's journey.

Donna's details are flavored with descriptive humor and vulnerability that make it possible for anyone to identify with her joys and challenges and find encouragement in how she was navigated by the God of the universe through both the road trip and the journey of life.

You will enjoy the book.

Jim Evans,
Senior Pastor
Heritage Alliance Church

DRIVING WITH THE LIGHT

My Spiritual Road Trip

BY

DONNA KRUEGER

Driving with the Light
Copyright © 2019 by Donna Krueger
All rights reserved

www.DonnaKrueger.com
donnakruegersbook@gmail.com
Facebook: Donna Krueger

Dedication

I dedicate this book to my brother Patrick J. Day. He was the first in our family to experience God's light and love and prayerfully directed the rest of us to it. He has been faithful to God by supporting missionaries all over the world and using his talents for God's Glory. At ninety-two he is still going strong and is a great example for how to live in your senior years.

Join me on my wonderful road trip adventure!

CONTENTS

FOREWARD

From the first time I met Donna Krueger, I was touched by the "light" that radiated from her. Her warm and cheerful personality, contagious faith, and the unconditional love she exuded attracted me to her. She shared with me about her desire to write this book and I was delighted that she was stepping out courageously to accomplish her dream even though the project was out of her comfort zone. I love the pioneer spirit that propels her.

I often meet those in the senior population who settle into complacency and wither away over the years in spirit, soul, and body, because they lack purpose and fresh vision. God wants us to dream big and pursue new opportunities all our days and Donna has found that key.

I love the way Donna leads the reader on a meaningful journey of revelation, inspiration, and truth as she shares her story. She parallels a challenging nine-month motor home trip with the obstacles, hardships, and tragedies, she experienced throughout her own life. I had no idea she had gone through all she did as there is not a hint of victim mentality on her when you meet her. She reminds me of when the three young Hebrew boys were thrown into the fiery furnace but when they came out there was not even a hint of fire or smoke on them.

Donna has chosen to discover the gold that was hidden in every hardship she lived through. Everyone has trials and painful situations in life, but some use these hard places as stepping-stones to greater opportunity and breakthrough while others unfortunately experience them as stumbling blocks. When you read *Driving with the Light*, you will be encouraged to receive healing for the hurts and trauma that have held you back and to stir your faith to engage in a glorious future. There are so many wonderful opportunities ahead of you no matter what situations your past has offered. It is time to move on. It is time to step into your best years ever.

Thank you, Donna, for this wonderful book. Bless you and blessings to all your readers! Well done!

Patricia King
Author, Television Host, Minister

PROLOGUE

I swung the front door open enthusiastically.

"I'm home!"

It was a Friday and I had spent the day at my State Rural Postal Carriers Convention. I was looking forward to going back that evening for the Luau Banquet with my husband.

"Gene, I'm *ho-ome!*" I called joyfully as I walked through the living room and into the family room.

Overwhelming silence greeted me.

Why isn't he answering me?

"Gene?" I took a few steps toward my husband in his easy chair and as he came into full view I gasped. Gene was slumped over, his face as white as a sheet. I immediately knew that, after forty-two years of life together, my beloved husband was no longer with me.

I checked his pulse just to be sure since my mind was having trouble keeping up with what was happening. It was my last clear thought before a cloud of shock and grief engulfed me. I came to the sudden realization that this was the beginning of some major changes in my life, and I asked God to please help me get through this.

I slowly reached for the phone and called 911. After that, I called Rick and Elva McNurlin because they are like my kids, and then I called a few close friends. The quick response team was there in five minutes, and shortly after there was a steady stream of people coming through the door. I stood by the kitchen counter confused and uncertain with a handful of friends surrounding me. I purposely separated myself from what was going on in the family room, but I had to be close because of all the questions.

What time did you find him?

Had he been sick?

I will need to have you sign this paper.

Would you like to keep his watch here?

What mortuary do you want him taken to?

How did I know? Gene was only sixty-eight and we had never discussed what mortuary we wanted to go to when we died. I was thankful to have my friends to talk with, and I hoped I was making the right choice.

Even through the fog of grief, I was keenly aware that my life had just changed forever.

Commit your works
to the Lord, and
your plans will be
established.

Proverbs 16:3

Chapter One

Journey of Commitment

jour·ney

/ˈjərnē/

noun
An act of traveling from one place to another

verb
Travel somewhere

My life journey began August 7, 1942, as the youngest of four children. My brothers, Pat and Joe, were fifteen and twelve, and my sister, Bobbie, was fourteen when I was born. I'm sure I was a surprise bundle of joy to my aging parents! My older two siblings left when I was very young and with my other brother often gone, I grew up as an only child. I was independent, resourceful, and received an abundance of love and attention. My mother faithfully took me to Sunday school and church. Singing about how Jesus loves me and listening to Bible stories were the beginning of my spiritual growth. With my Pollyanna personality, everything seemed good to me.

I was a small-town girl attending the local school, and I consider my teen years to have been fairly typical. As was very often the norm in those days, the end of my senior year in high school had me preparing to marry. On a warm, magical June day in 1960, I walked down the aisle to become the wife of Gene Krueger. I was young but thought I was grown up and ready to be an adult. As I look back, I had no idea about how hard the work was going to be and how much perseverance it was going to take to be a good farm wife and mother!

"First comes love, then comes marriage, then comes…" How well I remember that cold snowy December day in 1961 when I looked into my newborn daughter's little eyes as I held this miracle from God. I was concerned and fearful because she didn't come with an instruction manual, and I didn't know anything about being a mother! She managed to survive, and it wasn't long before David was born

Born: August 7, 1942

Siblings: 3

Married: June 1960

Children: Julie, David, Karma

and then a few years later, Karma. I loved being a mother and found this blessed journey to be gratifying and exciting, but also frustrating, with trials and unexpected challenges. And so, life went on, bringing with it ups and downs, joys and sorrows, good times and bad.

It had been ten days since Gene had passed away.

I was sitting at our big dining room table surrounded by endless piles of papers I had to fill out letting agencies know about Gene.

The business of death.

I was alone with my thoughts and it was hard to stay focused. A few days ago, I had been surrounded at this same table by my children and grandchildren talking and playing. Most of last week had been a blur of mortuary visits, a memorial service, and the spreading of his ashes. Wednesday had been particularly hard as I watched the older children clean out Gene's shop. I couldn't keep my mind from wandering back to the same date forty-two years ago when I walked down the aisle as a beautiful bride to say "I do" to the man I loved. What a full life of joys and sorrows we'd had together! Now it was ending with a memorial ceremony the next day.

I pulled my mind back to the job at hand. I had to get this paperwork done as I would be going back to work the next week.

For the last fourteen years, I had been a rural mail carrier in my small town of Kimberly. Yes, I was the lady driving the blue right-hand drive Subaru through the rain, wind, snow, and summer heat, putting mail into over 400 boxes each day. I really cared about my customers and enjoyed the work, but with Gene gone, how was I going to manage my demanding job and the enormous work of maintaining my property?

On a warm July afternoon, I turned into my driveway after an exhausting day of work, dreading all that I still needed to do at home. It had been only six weeks since Gene had passed away and I was in survival mode. After putting things away in the house, I trudged out to the irrigation ditch to start the pump. In the dry, arid high desert of southern Idaho, the garden and yard needed continual watering. As I pulled a hose around to the front yard so I could attach the circular sprinkler, I stopped and glanced around my place. The front lawn was framed on one side by two large weeping willow trees with graceful limbs that almost touched the ground. Many colorful flowers and roses surrounded my home.

It was such a beautiful place! But, *so* much work. I plodded around the house to the garden and started the water on the vegetables, berries, and fruit trees. Gene had planted the garden and now I was trying to keep it weeded and watered. He had loved keeping up our property, but the two acres were just too much for me. I glanced at the pasture full of weeds where our horses had once grazed on fresh green grass. I reached down and picked a ripe tomato and a cucumber before starting toward the house. As I passed the berries, I felt overwhelmed, knowing that after supper I would need to come back and pick a fair amount before I was done for the day. It would be another two months until the first frost, and I was wondering how I was going to survive until then. I would be sixty soon and I was exhausted all the time. I whispered, asking God to help me get through this challenging time. Little did I know about how He was planning to answer my prayer!

As I drove around on my country mail route, I did a lot of thinking and dreaming. What did I want my life to look like? What changes would I need to make? The only life I had ever known was that of a farm wife, never living more than four miles from my childhood home that my dad bought in 1916. The married life that I had grown to love came

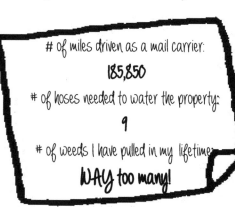

# of miles driven as a mail carrier:

185,850

# of hoses needed to water the property:

9

# of weeds I have pulled in my lifetime:

WAY too many!

to an abrupt end with my husband's passing. Our forty-two years of marriage had had its challenges, but we had made some great memories. When Gene died, I lost my best friend, confidante, companion, gardener, lover, and part-time cook.

I also lost my identity. I was no longer a wife. I was now a widow.

I struggled through the next two years adjusting to a new normal. It was convenient that I lived on my mail route because I could stop for lunch and let my schnauzer, Bo, outside since Gene was no longer there to do it. Our beautiful country home had taken years of arduous work and I loved it, but the reality was that it was way too much for me to care for on my own. However, I was surrounded by loving, caring friends and neighbors who were immensely helpful, especially after Gene passed away.

Was I ready to give all that up, or did I want to spend the rest of my life in Kimberly?

I finally made the commitment to sell my place and search for the new life God had for me. Since I love to travel, I decided what better way was there to pursue that life than a motor home road trip? If I was really serious about finding God's path, I needed to be brave and see what the world had to offer.

But starting a new adventure isn't always easy, and it took a lot of boldness and tenacity. I was going to be leaving the security I'd had my whole life in search of something new. I trusted that God had a special path for me, and I was eager to start looking for it once I made the choice. Still, I had so many questions and there were so many decisions to make! Where would I end up living? Would it be in another state? What should I keep, sell, or give away? I had no idea what the transition was going to look like, so my only choice was to put my full trust in God.

> *"Trust in the LORD with all your heart and lean not on your own understanding; in all your ways acknowledge Him, and He shall direct your paths."*
>
> *Proverbs 3:5-6*

My Spiritual Journey

Another life-changing commitment I made many years before became the foundation for my entire life journey. I had faithfully attended the United Methodist church my whole life. I participated in the youth group, attended summer camps and had been continually active in the church. I was married and all my children were baptized in that lovely church. I taught Sunday School, and I was sure I was a Christian because I was doing all the right things.

In the fall of 1969, our church scheduled a Lay Witness Mission weekend. Teams of fifteen to twenty parishioners would come for the weekend and stay in the homes of the congregation, then share their testimonies at the different meetings. Since this was supposed to be such a special event, my friend and I visited church members at home, encouraging them to attend.

I had no idea that this weekend would be completely life-changing for me.

This was the first Lay Witness Mission held in our area, and people came from all over the United States to share God's love. The meetings started on Friday evening, and after dinner, some of the visiting team gave their testimonies. They explained what their life had been like before asking Jesus into their life. They also related how their life had turned around after surrendering all to God. They all seemed to overflow with God's love. I was very familiar with the Bible verse:

"For God so loved the world that He gave His only begotten Son, that whoever believes in

Him should not perish but have everlasting life."

John 3:16

While they were sharing, that verse became so much more personal to me. God loved *me* so very much that He sent His one and only son to die for *me*. I had heard that verse so many times, but it wasn't until then that it really entered my heart. Jesus died for me!!!

We went to different homes for coffee and more sharing on Saturday morning, followed by a special luncheon. The people kept saying that all I needed to do was confess my sins, and He would forgive all of them and cleanse me.

"If we confess our sins, He is faithful and just to forgive us our sins and to cleanse us from all unrighteousness."

1 John 1:9

Those words kept going through my mind. As I took a deep, honest look at my life, I knew that I was far from perfect. There were many things I had done wrong. I hadn't been the best wife or mother. I complained and felt sorry for myself because my marriage wasn't the fairy tale I thought it would be. I had small and large sins. When I went home that Saturday afternoon, I knew that I wanted to confess my sins to God and ask Jesus into my life. When my children were resting in their rooms, I knelt by our worn brown couch nestled in the corner of our small living room and asked Jesus into my life.

I was so excited on Sunday morning because I wanted to make a public declaration of my new faith. As I made my way to the front, most of the church members were standing with me. This was a new revelation we had not heard before. I am sure there are still many people who go to church but haven't understood or experienced the freedom of God's salvation and light.

"And the light shines in the darkness, and the darkness did not comprehend it."

John 1:5

That weekend I realized that I truly had been walking in darkness, and it was the beginning of a fresh adventure along a newly lighted path. God had taken my husband out of the equation those few days because God had something special for me. Gene had spent the weekend deer hunting with friends. I couldn't wait until he got home so I could tell him the new truth I had discovered, and that Jesus was now living in me. I was sure that when he heard about the things I had learned, that he, too, would want to ask Jesus into his life. Well, that certainly wasn't the way it happened. He thought his wife had gone off the deep end and wasn't sure how to handle this new dynamic that had entered our relationship.

I was so enthusiastic about this new life that I was absorbing as much as I could from the Bible, books, and friends. God was still my main teacher, however. My first assignment was six months later when I learned the importance of being obedient to His nudging. When I heard that there was going to be a Lay Witness Mission in Nampa, Idaho, the Lord impressed on me that I should ask my older brother, Joe, to go. If you had known my brother, you would have said that there was *no way* he would go. Joe was forty years old, had never been married, had a drinking problem, and had not been in church since he was a youth. On Wednesday evening before the event, I went to his small bachelor pad and shared with him for the first time about how I had found a personal relationship with God. I told him about all the love that was given and received at the Lay Witness Mission event and asked if he would go with me. I remember him saying "No one loves me." I left him with Keith Miller's book, *The Taste of New Wine*. I asked him to read as much as he could and return it to me the next morning on his way to work, along with his decision. Standing in my kitchen the next morning, he was hesitant but said he would go. That was the first of many miracles.

We left early Saturday morning, dropped the children off at a friend's, and were back at the church in time to be assigned to a home for coffee. We attended the men's and ladies' luncheons at noon. After some free time in the afternoon, we returned for the evening potluck and more testimonies, then they divided us into small groups. The leader encouraged everyone to make a timeline of their spiritual walk. Joe's paper was blank. He told the leader that he had not experienced anything spiritual. She asked if he would like to change that and Joe said *yes*. That is when Joe gave his miserable, unsatisfying life to God.

I was so thankful that I had been obedient to the nudging of the Lord because I drove home the next afternoon with a new brother and someone who finally had some hope in his life. At home, he got rid of all his liquor and quit drinking. The next Sunday he went to prayer group, Sunday school, and church. Eventually, Joe started dating Sandie, the church organist, and a year and a half later they were married. He became an instant family man when he adopted her two children, Richard and Bea. They started going on Lay Witness Mission trips where Joe shared his story. I know there will be many people in heaven because of Joe's testimony.

Both my brother and I had been traveling in the dark. I had been involved in the church and thought I had the light, but I was missing the better things that God had for me. When people observed Joe's life, they knew he was living in the dark. In our journeys of life, we had been following our own plans, and taking many detours on the way. What we both found was the true light.

> *"Then Jesus spoke to them again saying, "I am the light of the world. He who follows Me shall not walk in darkness but have the light of life."*

John 8:12

Thirty-three years ago, asking Jesus to forgive my sins and take control of my life was a crucial decision. Now, I was looking at another decision and a journey into the unknown. I was very thankful that I was making this new decision with Jesus and that He would be with me no matter where I went or what happened because:

"He Himself has said, "I will never leave you nor forsake you."

Hebrews 13:5b

Here I am with my siblings. From left: Donna, Joe, Pat, and Bobbie, circa 1986.

Create in me a clean
heart, O God,
and renew a steadfast
spirit within me.

Psalm 51:10

Chapter Two

Passage to Freedom

By the time I retired in March of 2004, I had made the commitment to sell my home and travel. Right after the retirement party, I hit the ground running because of the enormous task of getting my home ready to sell. It was unbelievable how much stuff had accumulated in our long-married life! We had inherited antiques and possessions from both of our parents, as well as from a close relative we had taken care of. Both my husband and I were accumulators and not good at getting rid of things. To call us hoarders is a little strong, but you get the idea. My three-bedroom house had wall-to-wall furniture and the closets were overflowing. In addition to our full kitchen, we had a fruit room that we'd added on to hold all the canned food, supplies, and our two freezers. Gene had farmed and we had owned a lawn care business, so there was a large shop full of tools and equipment. He had taken up the hobby of woodworking and had saws and paraphernalia all over the shop. We had enjoyed camping, fishing, and hunting, so I had a boat, camping trailer, and hunting equipment.

One morning in prayer, I was thinking about my abundantly full home, so I asked God, "Please help me to get rid of the things I don't need any more." Well, you don't want to pray that prayer unless you really mean it! I had already asked my three children to come and take whatever they wanted. During the next few months, Julie came from Colorado, David from Michigan, and Karma from Nevada.

Wednesday morning before Memorial Day weekend, Julie, my oldest, and her friend, Linda, came to help with the *first* yard sale. As soon as Julie walked into the house, she handed me a package of sticky notes and told me to put them on what I wanted. Everything else would go. They were efficient, fast, and productive, and I was concerned they were pulling out things I was sure I couldn't live without.

Do I really have to get rid of the rustic end table my brother made in shop?

Don't get rid of all the unfinished craft projects and sewing stuff — I might want to finish those someday!

Do I have to take the time to go through all my books right now? Can't I just keep them and do it later?

Julie firmly told me that *later* was not an option.

I'm the kind of person that thinks, "I may need this someday." But their skillful and sometimes relentless organizational skills were just what I needed. They helped me let go of a lot of things, but in the moment, it was REALLY hard for me to see all my treasures gone or boxed up for the Salvation Army. God knew what I needed, though, and brought Julie and Linda to help me. That summer I probably got rid of 80% of my accumulated treasures. Not knowing what my future might hold, I put into storage what I thought I might need for a small two-bedroom apartment.

As I was diligently working on getting rid of clutter in my beloved home, I knew that I should start looking for the new home that would transport me around the United States. My trusted mechanic, Doug, said the best motor home would be a good used class C with a Ford engine, and low mileage. Of course, I wanted one that was clean and attractive. (Class C RVs have the small sleeping space above the cab, while Class As look like buses.) I researched several locally but none of them was what I wanted. In April, when I went to pick up my grandson, Skyler, from the Boise Airport, I thought it would be a fantastic opportunity to check out motor homes in that area. After a quick lunch, we began the search. We found a nice class C, and as my foot touched the soft green carpet and my eyes absorbed the plush green upholstery, accented by oak wood doors, I knew that this one was perfect for me. The beautiful bedroom in the back had a queen bed with closet space on each side and I liked the large bathroom with shower. Above the two seats in front was another bed and the table and bench seats could also be made into a bed. It was a 1993 Jayco Designer, which is the top of the line. The older couple selling it was going to quit the RV lifestyle. It came with EVERYTHING,

including a bike rack on the back, all the needed kitchen items, and even two small vacuums under the bed! The only thing I needed to do was to put my clothes and food in and I would be ready to go. I wasn't overly concerned about driving it myself, because I had been a farm wife and had driven large tractors and trucks, but I still sought advice from experienced RV owners.

I was always thinking about what my trip would look like, as I cleaned and fixed up my place each day. I had always found that the best part of any trip was planning and dreaming about the places I wanted to see. My good friends call me their "activities director" because I love to plan and organize trips and events. I bought an atlas of the United States, studied it, and then charted out where I would go and who I would see. I made a list of friends, school classmates, relatives, and ministry opportunities. I  decided to go across the northern states in the fall and then head south during the winter months. I mentally put a dot for each stop on the map and then connected them, until I had made a circle around the United States. I got so excited planning the trip and anticipating visiting people I had not seen for a long time! I was also looking forward to getting better acquainted with different areas of the country.

By far the hardest part of getting ready for the trip was clearing all the debris and clutter out of my place so new owners could move in. Planning the details of the trip was very time-consuming, but at least it was fun!

Imagine, if you will, a time long, long ago when people didn't have smartphones or GPS units…. When I embarked on my road trip in 2004, no one had these things. We were completely reliant on printed maps and flip phones. I know, I have no idea how we got around back then either! I used the atlas of the United States first to choose my overall route, then I went to the state maps to plot my path, then I got into the details of the small, inset maps for the specific cities of the places I planned to visit.

As long as I could avoid rush hour traffic, I should have no problems!

It's no secret that driving a big motor home is very different from driving a car.

No U-turns.

Backing up is hard.

You can't do anything quickly because the rig is just too big to maneuver that way.

The last thing you want to do is miss your freeway exit or take the wrong one because you'll waste a lot of time getting the rig turned around and back on the freeway so, before I entered a large city, I would stop at a rest area and memorize what highway and exit number would take me around the city. I also had a plan B in case I missed the exit. I made sure I paid close attention to the highway signs, constantly trying to confirm that I was on the correct road. As hard as I tried to be prepared, there were still so many times I found myself in the wrong place.

My
Spiritual
Journey

When I first accepted Christ into my life many years ago, I had that same enthusiasm for learning all I could about God, His love, and His life for me that I had for planning my trip. I even had my own map for my journey with Him—my Bible! I knew how important it was so I had it displayed on my coffee table so everyone could see and know that I was a Christian! Those first twenty-seven years I didn't read it much, although I kept it nicely dusted every week.

The people who had come for the Lay Witness Mission, had shared how they had such a hunger for the Bible and how it had come alive for them. I wanted to experience that same desire for God's word. One of the Bible translations that was popular then was the

Good News for Modern Man. This simple, easy-to-read version had just come out in paperback. It was great because I could highlight and write in it all I wanted to, with no worries about ruining my "good" Bible. Reading, meditating, and studying the Bible was very valuable because that is how I grew in my faith and developed a close relationship with God.

When I gave my life to God, there was the mess of past sins to clear out. Just like cleaning out my home, this also was a big job. I had been living for myself and wasn't happy with the life I had. As a busy young mother, however, I soon realized that growing in God was a process that takes weeks, months, and even years. I took care of some of the bigger sins the day I made my commitment but growing in our sanctification (creating that pure heart before the Lord) takes a while.

"Wash me thoroughly from my iniquity and cleanse me from my sin."

Psalm 51:2

God continually revealed hidden sins and as they surfaced, I confessed them, and He did the cleansing. Still, I would think a sin had been taken care of, but it would pop up later, often at a deeper level. I felt kind of like an onion—as I took one layer off, God would reveal the next. Even now, I find myself constantly asking God to cleanse me.

One of the problems God had been dealing with me about was control. I always liked to be in control of things. Being the youngest in my family, I'm sure I had everyone wrapped around my little finger and got pretty much what I wanted. Then I got married and tried to control my husband, family, and anything I might be associated with. There is a difference between being a leader and in charge of an activity and having a need to be in control

NOTE TO SELF: Stop trying to control everything!

of everyone and everything around you. Good leaders aren't controlling. The main thing to remember about control is making sure that you aren't trying to control something God doesn't want you to. We have to be able to take our hands off, and let God take care of things. He has had to work with me off and on through the years, but there is such freedom in realizing that I don't have to run everything!

In the same way that I had to completely rely on my maps when I was on the road trip, my Bible became the ultimate road map for my life. I would try really hard to follow the path that God had for me, but some sin or temptation would distract me, and I would end up on the wrong road. The closer my relationship with God became, the sooner I would realize my mistake and backtrack until I got back on the right path. As God has been my guide and the light I follow, He and my Bible have helped me along one step at a time, day after day, year after year. I could never have gotten to where I am now without Him! It is one of the most precious gifts I have ever received. I discover hidden mysteries all the time, and it is a treasure chest of information for living well. As I meditate on different verses, the Holy Spirit breathes life into my soul.

> *"Your Word is a lamp to my feet and a light to my path."*
>
> *Psalm 119:105*

The Bible has the answer to any situation that you might be facing. Over the years, I have learned the value of memorizing Bible verses. Not only has it been helpful as I was doing it, but those verses have been there for me my whole life in times of crisis or when God wanted me to give an encouraging word to someone. The most exciting thing to me is that the Bible is God's love letter to me.

Preparing for the trip was exciting and fun. I had a wonderful time looking for the right motor home, studying the maps, and planning my trip. But parts of it were very painful, like cleaning out, selling my home, and leaving behind so many friends and memories. Just like life – there are good and bad sides to almost everything.

The best part of the journey for me was the anticipation of what was ahead. I looked forward to all the time I would have to spend with family and friends and, of course, all the time I would have alone with my best friend Jesus. He was and is very precious to me.

It has been fifteen years since I took that trip and I still have the same excitement and anticipation about what God has ahead for me! It doesn't matter how old you are; He still wants us to be willing workers who will be faithful in carrying out His plans for this world.

Our house on Falls Avenue

The garden.

Be anxious for nothing, but in everything by prayer and supplication, with thanksgiving, let your requests be made known to God; and the peace of God, which surpasses all understanding, will guard your hearts and minds through Christ Jesus.

Philippians 4:6-7

Chapter Three

The Smashing Beginning

The day had finally come! Time to embark on my big journey.

After the many weeks I had spent clearing out my house, I was exhausted. But I was determined to get going that day, September 17th, because my daughter in Larkspur, Colorado wanted me to meet some of her friends from church on Sunday and then she was leaving that Wednesday on a business trip. To make that happen, I had to leave on time.

How many of you can relate to the process of moving out of your house? There's that moment where you think everything is finally done and you've waved goodbye to the moving truck in the driveway, but when you turn around and trudge back into the house, it's still a mess? In addition, there are little things that didn't pack well scattered all over the house? Well, in my situation, not only was I leaving the house forever, but I also had to think about what I would need for my very long trip. Try though I did, I didn't get everything perfectly matched up into the Storage and Motorhome categories. I had also been so busy with the big move that I still had a lot of last-minute things that I needed to do. As I checked each thing off my list, I kept shoving (and I do mean SHOVING) things into my motor home because I wasn't sure what I would need. I seemed to have forgotten for the moment that I wasn't taking a road trip to the deepest, darkest parts of the Amazon jungle where there wouldn't be a grocery store or a Target every ten miles.

My trip FINALLY started around 4:00 p.m. when I climbed into my overstuffed RV to begin my nine-month journey. I made a brief stop at a campground to get rid of the wastewater and sewage, so it was closer to 5 p.m. before I left the area. But I'm nothing, if not persistent; I had said I was going to leave on the 17th and that meant that I was *going* to leave on the 17th.

My first stop was to be at the home of some friends in Evanston, Wyoming. Driving by car would have only taken four hours, but it took an extra few in the big rig. I was so happy to finally be on my way! I made it to their home before 10 p.m. I was completely exhausted from the last few days, so I didn't visit very long before turning in. The next morning, I wanted to stay a little longer to catch up with my school friend, but I needed to get to my daughter's that evening. It was a little after 10:00 a.m. when I merged back onto I-80 to spend the day singing with my worship music and enjoying the sunny skies of Wyoming. Most of the day, I drove through the desolate southern part of the state. I saw a whole lotta nothing, punctuated by some antelope gracefully grazing in the range land.

It was just God and me going on this journey together, so I was sharing my excitement and anticipation with the Lord, talking to Him about how much I was looking forward to all the hours we would be spending with each other as I drove. I was also really looking forward to visiting family and friends. It was late afternoon before I turned south and headed for the Colorado border.

A little after dark, I entered Fort Collins, Colorado. I wasn't sure if the highway I was on would take me to I-25, so I thought I had better pull into a gas station to check my map. Because it was dark and I couldn't see exactly where the entrance to the gas station was, I turned too soon and ended up in the back of a motel. As I considered my surroundings, I saw rows of cars parked in front of the guests' rooms. I thought the best and safest thing to do would be to go around to the front entrance and turn back on the highway from there. As I approached the front of the motel, I saw the cement island that marked the area where cars could pull up to register their arrival. I carefully maneuvered to the left side, since there were cars parked on the right, cheerfully thinking that I'll correct this little detour and be back on the highway before I knew—

The loud crashing of metal crunching against a solid object interrupted my thoughts. It's times like this when you have 100 things go through your mind in a matter of seconds. I had just been trying to not bother anyone and quietly sneak out of the motel parking area and suddenly everyone was coming out of their rooms to see what had caused the thundering noise that had broken the silence of the evening! A man standing on the balcony of the second floor was pointing to the sign with a number that gave the height restrictions.

Thanks, buddy. Obviously, I hadn't seen it, or I'd be on my way to Larkspur by now. I hadn't even had the first thought about the awning that went across the entrance to the hotel or that I was now driving a much taller vehicle than my little Subaru.

My second great idea was *little* and take inventory of the crashing I heard when I drove compared to the scraping and happened when I backed up. detached itself from the top of to just back up a damage. The in was nothing screeching that The awning finally my vehicle, landing at a jaunty downward slope, like the bunny run at a ski resort.

I'll just back up a *little...*

By this point, I had given up on the idea that I would be able to just pop back onto the highway anytime soon. Sure enough, what must have been the *entire* fire and police departments of this small town pulled in, lights and sirens blaring to beat the band.

They were all very handsome and helpful. Eventually, all the hotel guests went back to bed. When I got a chance, I called my daughter and through many tears, explained my situation. She was thankful that I wasn't hurt, unlike the top of my motor home. She reassured me that the insurance would take care of the damages, but little did she know. The ordeal over the repairs was a nightmare story for another day!

Oh, *all right*. I'll tell you now. To make a three-year story short, the hotel inflated their bill so much when they submitted it to the insurance company that the whole mess ended up in court. The hotel won the judgment (which was more than I got from the sale of my house and farm acreage!) Because I was on the road and moved a few times during those year, I had no idea what had happened until the insurance company managed to track me down and sued me for $68,000. It took months of negotiating, but we finally settled on $10,000 just to get it over with.

The hotel never did replace the awning.

Back to my story:

After the investigation of the accident was finished, I had to decide if I was going to continue to drive the 110 miles to my daughter's home or find a place where I could pull over for the night. I asked the policeman if my motor home was drivable. After checking it over, he said that the main problem would be the folding TV antennae that was now NOT attached to the roof and was dangling by the cord. He said that he could cut it off for me, which he did, and then laid it to rest on the bed, which pretty well committed me to driving the 110 miles. There I was, exhausted and emotionally drained, an elderly woman limping slowly down I-25 in an injured motor home.

I finally made it to Julie's just before midnight.

Did I have second thoughts about continuing with this long motor home excursion? Not really. In my life there had been many unexpected trials and most of the time, I found that good things came out of them.

"And we know that all things work together for the good to those who love God, to those who are the called according to His purpose."

Romans 8:28

While they were putting a new roof, awning, and air-conditioner on my motor home, I was able to get a much-needed rest from the arduous weeks of getting my home ready for the new owners. I enjoyed the extra time with my daughter before and after her business trip. I had a close school friend who lived in Pueblo, so I borrowed my daughter's car and spent two lovely days with Beverly and her family, who took me on a day trip into some of the beautiful mountains of Colorado.

In my quest to find the new life God had for me, I researched Christian ministries in the Colorado Springs area. I was able to visit several that were headquartered there, including Focus on the Family, The Navigators, and YWAM (Youth with a Mission). I loved every minute of seeing firsthand what these wonderful ministries were doing but didn't feel any pull from the Lord that I was to be involved with any of them.

Upwards and onwards, as they say!

After a two-week rest at Julie's, my RV was ready to roll. The outside looked great, with a new awning and air conditioner. The inside…well, not so much. If you had seen it, you would have been able to confirm that I had definitely overpacked.

Julie to the rescue again! She set up tables outside and we put everything on them. We cleaned and purged and only put back in what I would need for the rest of my trip.

My
Spiritual
Journey

Just like my first two days of travel, we'd had some trying times in our life in Idaho. When Gene and I were first married, he was employed on a farm because he always enjoyed working with the soil and seeing things grow. He worked for Howard Gardner, who was a distant relative. When Howard decided to retire in 1974, he sold us the equipment and we leased the 450 acres of irrigated land that Howard had farmed. The main crops we grew were seed beans, seed peas, hay, and a variety of grains. After we'd had two years of good crops, we bought a new Ford pick-up in the fall of 1975. In January, we put a down payment on our first home. The next August, less than a month before the crops were to be harvested, a large hailstorm pelted just about every one of the fields we farmed. It cost us around $20,000 in lost income. We were trying to get caught up from that when the farm prices started to decline.

The crash happened on August 30, 1982. Gene had just started to cut and rake the beans as it was the beginning of the fall harvest. We owned a big CB Hayes combine and, besides threshing our own beans, we had a small business threshing for other farmers. The CB Hayes was an enormous orange combine pulled by a large tractor. It had a giant metal bin high on one side that the seed was put into and then it was dumped into a truck that pulled under the bin to catch it.

That morning Gene had been out checking the water in the fields. Our daughter, Karma's, palomino horse needed to be taken to the veterinarian because the county fair was starting that week. Our children were very involved in 4-H, so fair time was a busy, important activity for us. My kitchen counters were covered with mason jars and boxes of peaches lined the floor ready for a day of canning. I stopped what I was doing and helped Gene load Nugget into the trailer.

After the veterinarian had taken care of her and we started to get into the pickup, Gene asked if I would drive, since he was not feeling well. Just as I turned the pickup on to the main road and started the four-mile trip to our house, Gene said he thought he was having a heart attack. He told me exactly what to do as soon as we got home. He would go into the house while I unloaded the horse and put her in the pasture, and then I was to call 911. Later, when I thought about it, I knew that I should have called 911 immediately, but I had learned a long time ago that I needed to do things just like he told me.

The ambulance finally came, and I remember as I was driving to the hospital, I was repeating a Bible verse I had memorized:

> *"Be anxious for nothing, but in everything by prayer and supplication, with thanksgiving, let your requests be made known to God; and the peace of God, which surpasses all understanding, will guard your hearts and minds through Christ Jesus."*
>
> *Philippians 4:6-7*

This verse proved to be extremely helpful during the following weeks. Gene had to spend the next three days in intensive care from the heart attack. Just like the crash that happened with my motor home, this happened very abruptly and wasn't part of the day's planned activities.

I've noticed that accidents never seem to happen at a good time.

Our son, David, who had just gone to the University of Idaho to start his second year of college, decided to drive the eight hours back home to help with the harvest. We had wonderful neighbors who took time from their own farms to cut and rake our beans so they could start the drying process and be ready to thresh. David's best friend, Rick McNurlin, was still going to school at CSI, our local junior college, and he helped as much as he could. I even had friends who took the peaches and jars and canned them for me. Most of my next few days were spent between the hospital and the fairgrounds, where I helped Karma show her horse and sheep.

Just as I had to make some adjustments to my travel plans, we had to make some adjustments back on the farm. The bean harvest lasted five to six weeks if the weather cooperated. Between David staying for two weeks, the help of Rick and John (our hired man), and some neighbors, we managed to make it through. I helped a bit with driving trucks, but one of my main jobs was to keep Gene off the combine. He was supposed to be resting and recuperating but keeping him away from the fields was next to impossible. He thought he needed to drive his pickup out there and be available for any supervision that might be required. Then he slowly started doing some of the work. Ever since we had bought the combine nine years before, it was my job to cook a hot meal and take it to the combine crew every evening. This year was no exception. In my "spare" time, I was canning and freezing produce from our garden. How did we make it through times like that? I know that many prayers were being said for us, and I don't know how we would have made it without God's help. He gives us the strength and fortitude to endure such trying times, and it is through these experiences that we seem to grow the most spiritually.

I was continuing to grow in my Christian walk. As I studied the Bible, I grew in my love relationship with God. I wanted to learn and continue growing as fast as I could, so I dove into various activities. I was involved in the church and Bible studies and enjoyed reading various testimonies of well-known Christian leaders. I surrounded myself with Christian friends who had the same desires as I did. It is important to surround yourself with people who have the same goals and values that you have. The first few years after I had invited Christ into my life, I traveled to different towns and became part of the Lay Witness Mission teams. It was during this time that I began to learn more about the Holy Spirit.

> *"We are free to live, not according to our flesh,*
> *but by the dynamic power of the Holy Spirit."*
>
> *Romans 8:4b (TPT)*

I wanted to know more about the dynamic power of the Holy Spirit. When I asked Jesus to come into my life, I got the whole thing: God (the Father), Jesus (the son), and the Holy Spirit. I had the Holy Spirit in me but didn't realize that there was more to having relationship with him. Just before Jesus was to leave His disciples for the last time, He came into the midst of them and said:

> *"'Peace to you! As the Father has sent Me, I*
> *also send you' And when He had said this, He*
> *breathed on them and said, 'Receive the Holy*
> *Spirit."*
>
> *John 20:21-22*

When Jesus breathed on them, it was the breath of life of the Holy Spirit. In the beginning of Acts, Jesus commanded them not to leave Jerusalem but to "wait for the Promise of the Father" (Acts 1:4c). He knew that they wouldn't be able to continue with the ministry of spreading the Gospel without the power of the Holy Spirit.

> *"For John truly baptized with water, but you*
> *shall be baptized with the Holy Spirit not*
> *many days from now."*
>
> *Acts 1:5*

"But you shall receive power when the Holy Spirit has come upon you; and you shall be witnesses to Me, in Jerusalem, Judea and Samaria, and to the ends of the earth."

Acts 1:8

The disciples congregated with many of Jesus' followers in the upper room in Jerusalem. They had no idea what to expect but did what Jesus told them to do. This was one big prayer meeting (about 120 were there)!

"These all with one mind were continually devoting themselves to prayer."

Acts 1:14 (NASB)

This prayer time and fellowship went on for several days, until Pentecost, the tenth day after the ascension of Jesus, when the Holy Spirit came upon them.

"And suddenly there came a sound from heaven, as of a rushing mighty wind, and it filled the whole house where they were sitting. Then there appeared to them divided tongues, as of fire, and one sat upon each of them. And they were all filled with the Holy Spirit and began to speak with other tongues, as the Spirit gave them utterance."

Acts 2:2-4

Something special happened that day of Pentecost that changed their lives forever. The Power of the Holy Spirit fully immersed them, and they were "baptized" with the Holy Spirit. The Spirit came with nine gifts:

Gifts of tongues

Interpretation of tongues

Prophecy

Word of knowledge

Word of wisdom

Discerning of spirits

Faith

Healing

Miracles

When I discovered that those same gifts could be for me, I knew that I wanted all that God had promised me. The Holy Spirit is God's presence within us. He is the very spirit of God.

That was forty-seven years ago, and it has been a wonderful journey that has included many valleys, hilltop experiences, and of course, rough roads. I have learned so much more about the Holy Spirit as He has continually been with me through all the wonderful journeys I have been on.

The inside of my overstuffed RV before the second purge.

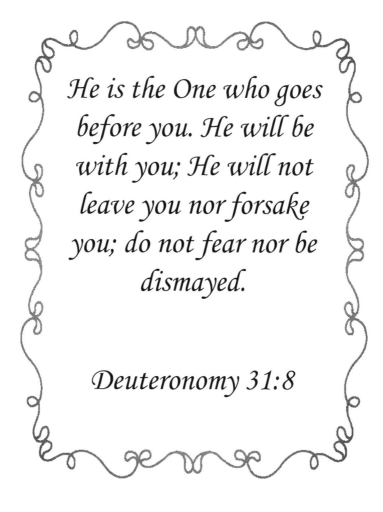

He is the One who goes before you. He will be with you; He will not leave you nor forsake you; do not fear nor be dismayed.

Deuteronomy 31:8

Chapter Four

The Route Through the Storm

It was now Wednesday, October 6th, and, after experiencing seventeen days of forced rest and relaxation, I was raring to get back to my adventure. As I pulled out of the driveway, I marveled at the beauty of the fall colors all around. I glanced in my rearview mirror to see my daughter waving goodbye and probably saying a little prayer for safe travels for her adventurous mother.

I needed to send two boxes of the things we had cleaned out of the motor home back to Idaho, so I stopped at the Post Office. When I got back to the rig, I did a quick walk-around, which I had been taught to do in my mail carrying days. I looked at the back, right duel tire and I couldn't believe my eyes. The tire had been cut by something! Maybe a rock in Julie's driveway? I had no idea how it happened, but there was a slash in the tire that hadn't been there earlier.

I was so disappointed!

I called Julie, who looked up the closest Big O Tires. She found one in Castle Rock, Colorado and gave me the directions. She said she had noticed as I was driving away that the back end looked especially low, but she figured it was just all the books we'd stuffed under the bed in the back room. She suggested that I move them to the storage units in the middle of the vehicle and put lighter things under the bed. I have a whole new respect for the baggage loaders at the airport. Where you put things in a moving vehicle matters! I was only on my second day of living and driving my home-on-wheels, so I guess making rookie mistakes was understandable.

Good news: I found the tire dealership!

Bad news: Neither they, nor any of the other local stores, had the tire I needed.

Good news: After kindly calling around for me, keeping my route in mind, they found one in Columbia, Missouri!

Bad news: I was going to have to drive through the rest of Colorado, all of Kansas, and half of Missouri on a spare.

You can be sure that I asked the Lord to keep that tire up and running until I could buy a new one!

With the delays at the tire store, I didn't get to the eastern side of Colorado until dark. I was tired and didn't want to drive much longer, so Julie found a campground for me just before the Kansas state line. When she was available, she was my GPS many times during the trip, but she traveled a lot with her job, so my son, David, was next on the list to call, then my daughter, Karma. After that, it was anyone who would answer their phone. I had one of those old flip phones, but at least I had one, if I was fortunate to be somewhere where there was service.

After a good night's rest, I was ready for my next day of travel. My goal was to get through Kansas. I had a little talk with God and mentioned that I would sure appreciate it if there would be no problems with my RV that day. I put on my praise music, and the Lord and I had a good time together. It's a long way across Kansas, but being a farm wife, I enjoyed driving through their agricultural land. Some people say that the drive through Kansas is not very interesting, but if you look for God's beauty, you can find it anywhere. I'm sure there are people who drive through southern Idaho and say it is a pretty desolate country. However, when you get off the interstate, there is a lot of hidden beauty to be found in its rivers, canyons, and mountains.

As I was approaching Kansas City, I was thinking through my options. It would be nice if I could get to the other side of the city, then I wouldn't have to experience the rush hour traffic in the morning. Someone had told me there was a big Walmart on the other side of Kansas City where I could park to spend the night. Walmart allows people to stay in their lots in some parts of the country.

I glanced around and noticed that the clouds were getting darker by the minute. After I managed to get to the other side of the city, I saw a few raindrops falling on my window. Now, all I had to do was find the Walmart. I took an exit that I *thought* might be a possibility, but it turned into a residential area, so back to the freeway I went. It would have been so easy if I had been taking that trip now; I'd just Google "Walmart" and be on my way! I asked God to please help me find where I should spend the night. After passing a few exits, I decided I would take the next one. The rain was coming down harder and it seemed like this might be another dead end. Just then, the road made another bend and there is it was in the middle of a row of stores.

Number of Walmarts in Kansas City:

7

A Walmart!!!!

I don't think it was the big Walmart I'd been told about, but it was a Walmart. At the back of the parking lot there were a few other motor homes, so I went over and parked by them. Just as I set the parking brake, the whole heavens opened up! If I hadn't known better, I would have thought I was parked under a waterfall. I don't know if I had ever experienced such a heavy rainfall in my life.

After a very full day of traveling, I was exhausted. I didn't even turn my inside lights on, because the light in the parking lot was bright enough. I quickly fixed a peanut butter and jam sandwich and went right to bed.

When I woke up the next morning to blue sunny skies, I was delighted, after falling asleep with the pelting rain crashing down on my roof. I told God how thankful I was to be in a secure place before the worst of the storm hit. I was looking forward to the relief I was going to feel when I got a new tire that day, so I didn't have to worry about the spare holding up. Thankfully, it wasn't a very long drive to Columbia, Missouri.

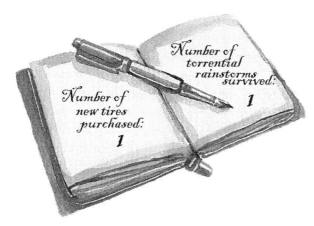

As I was driving east on the interstate, I noticed all the bad accidents that had happened the night before. Not only were there cars off the road and in the median, but also large semi-trucks. I said another thank you to God for my safety the night before.

While I was having lunch, waiting for the new tire to be put on, I experienced the humidity of the Midwest! This was something new for me coming from the high desert in Idaho. The temps might get above 100 degrees in the summer, but as they say, "it was a *dry* heat."

58

I was very pleased to have enjoyed my first day of uneventful, relaxing travel! The reason I chose to come to northeastern Illinois was that I wanted to take a little time and research my great-grandfather, George Clay Day. He had grown up in Fountain County, close to Attica, Indiana. My overnight stop was just across the border.

After an early breakfast, I drove the short distance to Attica. I was able to find the land where George lived, imagining what it would have looked like 150 years ago. I was extremely fortunate to be able to find the cemetery (in the middle of a field) where his parents and grandparents were buried. At that time, I was the family member who had most of the historical information on our ancestors. I saw in this trip a wonderful opportunity to do some "boots on the ground" research.

I wasn't planning to spend too much time on this little side trip because I was anxious to get to my son's home in Michigan. I meandered on country roads, working my way across Indiana to interstate I-60. From there, it was a hop, skip, and a jump to Haslett, Michigan, where I would be spending the rest of October.

As I finally turned into my son's driveway in Haslett, Michigan, I took a minute and contemplated all that had taken place in a little less than a month and pondered what the future held. What would my visit in Michigan look like? What did God have for me here? Would this be the state where I would find my final destination?

My Spiritual Journey

I had been sure, on that beautiful fall morning in Colorado, that I was ready to really get going on my adventure. I had felt the same way after Gene's heart attack, and the crops had been harvested, and he had finally been able to get some rest. I was confident that our life was ready for the next part of our journey. Just as I had discovered the unexpected cut in the tire soon after I started my road trip, it wasn't too long before I saw the slash in our lives that would interfere with what I had hoped would be getting back to normal.

After the hail in 1976, the farm prices continued to drop, and the interest rates were skyrocketing. Each spring, the bank would loan us what we thought we would need for operating expenses that year, but we were not able to always pay the loan off. Part of the problem was the country was going through a severe economic recession. The prime interest rate had hit an all-time high of 21.5% in June of 1982. When Gene went to the bank in March of 1983, they informed us that, if things didn't turn around for the better, that this would be the last year they would loan us money. This meant that we were running on thin ice. We would have to tighten our belts and cut expenses as much as we could.

Gene's heart and body seemed to be healing well, but his mental condition was another story. He had always had some problems with depression, but now, with the possibility that he would have to give up farming, the dark cloud of feeling like a failure settled over him. All he had wanted to do since he was in school was to farm. The first of April, I finally talked him into going to the doctor because something had to change. The doctor put him on antidepressants. However, it takes time to find out what medicine works best, and Gene wasn't very patient, so he didn't work with the doctor to find the best one.

It was time to work in the fields and get them ready for planting, but because Gene was depressed, it was an effort to even get out of the house. I thought it was good therapy for him to get back into the fields, but he wasn't able to do it all himself. Rick McNurlin, who has been like a son to us, was still at CSI. When he wasn't busy with school he helped on the farm. I spent more time on the tractors and working to get the fields ready to plant. I would leave the field at 11:30 a.m., go home and fix lunch for everyone, and then head back to the field after lunch. We were in a position where we couldn't afford to hire extra help, so we did as much as we could ourselves. When you are a farm wife and there is work to do, you roll up your sleeves and "git 'er done." One fall, the engine went out on the big CB Hays combine. It needed to be fixed as soon as possible because there were beans in the field that needed to be harvested. Gene knew the fastest and only way to get it overhauled was to do it himself. I spent all night holding a flashlight and being the mechanic's helper until it was ready to run.

That summer of 1983 felt like a marathon. It was a great blessing when my sister, Bobbie, and her husband Lee, came and lived with us for six weeks. Lee enjoyed working in the fields and was a big help to Gene, while Bobbie was able to help around the house. They wouldn't take any money and considered their room and board enough. I certainly enjoyed the time we had together. Our son David was working at the United States Department of Agriculture Research Service each summer to help pay for college, but David and Rick helped out whenever they could. We managed to get through the summer and harvest the crops.

Still, just like when I observed the clouds getting darker in Kansas, I could see the atmosphere around our home continuing to get darker. Even with the hours of hard work and cutting the corners as much as we could, it still wasn't good enough. When you lease the land, the owners get 50% of the profits, so when prices fall, you don't end up making very much.

When Gene went to the bank on November 15th, 1983, the bank officers strongly suggested that we sell all our equipment and quit farming. They thought if we did it then, there would be enough money from the sale of everything to pay all we owed them. We had known, deep down, that it was coming, but it wasn't until they finally said, "this is the end" that it really struck home. Just like in Kansas City when the storm hit its peak and the blinding rains came down, something like this smacks you so hard that your mind hits pause, and it is difficult to function.

I woke up on the morning of February 23, 1984, with anticipation but it wasn't like the excited feeling I'd had when I knew I was going to get the new tire. That day in 1984, the anticipation was made up of sorrow, sadness, apprehension, fear, and anxiety. We had been getting ready for our farm sale for several weeks and today was the day. I was very thankful to see the sun glistening on the snow-covered ground. Our sale was one of the first of the season, so we had been concerned about the weather. The two days before, there hadn't been much we could do but pray as we watched the large snowflakes keep falling. Finally, the day of the sale, the weather cleared, and we appreciated all the people who came to help to scrape away the snow around the lines of equipment and the parking area. We were very thankful to see farmers come from all over the valley, and at the same time, very sad to see the equipment we had spent so many hours on slowly leave with another owner. We took in enough money to pay what we owed the bank, but the amount above that was very minimal. We wondered if it would it be enough to establish us on the next part of our life journey.

That spring in Idaho found us researching what kind of job Gene would be able to do. After a couple of months and lots of prayer, we decided to go into the lawn care business. I always said that Gene just traded his big tractor in for a smaller one, and instead of going up and down large fields, he was going back and forth across green grass, giving it a weekly haircut. Did you notice I said we? Yes, I knew that it was going to be work we would have to do together. If you haven't been able to tell by now, I was an enabler. I put all my efforts into trying to save the farm and that didn't work. Now, I needed to "Stand by My Man" and help him get this new business operating efficiently. We had arrived at a new destination on our journey, and I was praying that this was where God wanted us.

The spiritual road trip I was on around this time seemed to be very rough and filled with potholes, with a few refreshing activities. One of the things I enjoyed the most was being part of Christian Women's Luncheons, sponsored by Stonecroft. I started in the mid-'70s by attending and leading a small neighborhood Bible Study. I have always loved introducing people to Jesus, so they could enjoy the same friendship with Him that I did. It still thrills me to be able to teach and mentor people into a closer, more intimate relationship with Him! I had the honor and privilege of serving as an officer and even did a little speaking. During this time, I made some life-long friend-ships. After the farm sale, we were tired and emotionally drained, but it was so refreshing when two ladies from CWC brought dinner over with butterfly stickers all over the packages to represent new begin-nings. I was so thankful for this support!

While all my energy had been going into trying to save the farm and then starting a new business, Gene was still being weighed down by different levels of depression. All of this was very draining for me. I was on my own roller coaster of emotions and questions in my spiritual life. One day I would write in my journal: "Life is really the pits; I don't know how I am going to survive." A few days later, I would thank God for the encouragement I received from various individuals. For some of you who have experienced living with someone who is depressed, you'll understand that it is not fun. I am basically a positive person, but after a while, I became worn down with the effort of trying to help him. My own life was being depleted of joy, fun, laughter and any other positive emotion I might have. It got so bad that I ended up going into depression myself. On the outside, I was functioning and doing things that needed to be done, but on the inside, I knew I wasn't myself. This went on for a year or two.

For those of you who have gone through some these same feelings, let me explain how my healing happened. I had been spending most of my time trying to help my husband at the expense of myself. I had stopped Christian Women's Luncheons and Bible studies. About the only thing I continued to do was go to church. I wasn't doing much for me. I had many people praying for me, so looking back, I could see how God's hand was in all of this. On November 22, 1985, some ladies at a Woman's Aglow meeting prayed for the depression to go away. Some prayers are answered right away, but sometimes the healing comes over a period of time. Healing from my depression took a long time. God put circumstances in my life to show me that I needed to take an active part in making some changes.

After college, Julie got a job with Micron in Chandler, Arizona. Early in 1986, she finally was able to get a home of her own and she wanted me to come to Arizona and help her decorate it. She had worked hard for a degree in Electrical Engineering but had no knowledge of how to create a comfortable, attractive home. I went and enjoyed changing her house into a beautiful home over the course of ten days. Being able to step away and out of my home environment gave me the ability to see that there was a better life out there, and I didn't want to continue being stuck in the same ruts. Sometimes, you have to get away from your situation in order to get a good look at how bad things are. It was like there was a large, dark cloud of depression over our home. It wasn't until I got away and experienced some wonderful light that I realized how dark my life had become.

When I got home, I knew I needed to make some deliberate choices. I chose to not continue to feel sorry for myself, to stop focusing on my circumstances, and to do something to make my life better. I researched and found a good prayer and support group and went to that on a regular basis. I made a point of spending more time with God. I enjoyed a movie or night out with my girlfriends. I chose joy. I chose to think good thoughts and to meditate on Bible verses like:

> *"Finally, brethren, whatever things are true, whatever things are noble, whatever things are just, whatever things are pure, whatever things are lovely, whatever things are of good report, if there is any virtue and if there is anything praiseworthy—meditate on these things."*

> *Philippians 4:8*

I had been murmuring and complaining, forgetting where that had gotten the Israelites after they left Egypt. Forty years in the desert, that's what they got. Well, I had been in a dry desert long enough and I was ready to enter into a land of milk and honey—my promised land.

It was eleven months after they had prayed for my healing that I finally started to see some improvement. My journal entry for September 21, 1986, read:

> *Thank you, God, for the emotional healing that has been taking place in my life. It has been slowly going on since November of last year. There have been lots of ups and downs, but it has been a gradual uphill trend. I know that the trials help me grow and I hope I have learned from them.*

As Gene and I started the new business, we reflected on the last few years. Our first choice had been to farm, but the reality was that the farming lifestyle was behind us. We needed to look forward to the future and find the path that God had for us. I also reflected on my spiritual journey. I had taken some small, but significant, steps and

65

I was continually trying to stay focused on what God wanted me to do and to become the women He had designed me to be.

Our lawncare business equipment.

The LORD is near to
those who have a
broken heart,
And saves such as have
a contrite spirit.

Psalm 34:18

Chapter Five

Unexpected Avenues to Wholeness

I was thrilled to have arrived at my son's house in Michigan. Because of living so far away, I hadn't been able to spend as much time with my grandchildren as I wanted to, so I enjoyed a marvelous weekend playing cards and games with Alexis (10), Emma (7), and Matthew (4) and enjoying my son, David and his wife, Cammie. Early Monday, I called my friend Bobbie, who lived with her husband, Dutch, on Cook Lake. They were in the middle of Hiawatha Forest, located in the Upper Peninsula of Michigan, or as locals say, UP. She said the fall trees were at their peak of color and she encouraged me to come as soon as I could. My grandchildren were in school during the week and my son and Cammie worked so I decided I would leave the next morning.

Early Tuesday morning found me singing along with Willie Nelson:

"On the road again! I can't wait to get on the road again!"

I would put this on every time I started the next leg of the trip. David and his family lived in Haslett, Michigan, close to East Lansing. To get to the Upper Peninsula, I just headed north. The bright red, yellow, orange, and rust leaves on the trees that framed highway were stunning. David said that October was his favorite month because of the beautiful fall foliage.

I crossed the massive Mackinac Bridge, which some people call the Mighty Mac, enjoying beautiful views of Lake Michigan on the left and Lake Huron on the right. It got its name because it is the third largest suspension bridge in the US and one of the world's longest bridges overall. It's 26,372 feet, which makes it close to five miles long, and has four lanes of traffic. It was impressive.

As my tires rolled onto the soil of the Upper Peninsula, my whole being was anticipating the beauty that was awaiting me. I was amazed at the number of deciduous trees with their crimson colors covering the rolling hills. God must have had so much fun creating this majestic autumn masterpiece! The whole horizon was a fantastic display of color as far as you could see. Trees dressed in their assorted colors reflected magnificently on the small lakes that dotted the landscape. The forests of Idaho display beautiful fall colors, but the mountains consist mostly of evergreen trees. This was miles and miles of brilliant, stunning color.

I was able to find their place (no easy task because it was so far out in the country). For the next three days, Bobbie showed me magnificent sights in her little corner of the world. I saw the colorful picture rocks along Lake Superior. The waterfalls in that area were beautiful. Munising, Wagner and Alger Falls were each unique in their own charming way. We spent some time around Grand Island Harbor and watched the birds on the sandy beach. We took a day and went to the delightful city of Escanaba, where Bobbie spends some of her time golfing. In the evening we would travel through the colorful forest to quaint restaurants on an exquisite lake with a gorgeous view. I didn't even mind the few scattered rain showers because I relished the smell of the fresh rain that glistened on the roads. Many friends have asked me what the most beautiful area was I saw. It's hard to choose, but the upper peninsula of Michigan may well have been it!

It was nice to have my own home and bed with me during this stay, but I also thoroughly enjoyed having someone drive me around in their car so I could enjoy the scenery and not worry about what road to take.

My marvelous time in the Upper Peninsula had come to an end. Sitting at the table on Saturday morning, eating my morning fruit and cereal, I looked above the mass of red- and gold-leaved trees and saw storm clouds gathering in the west.

Uh oh.

How might this storm affect my trip home? Would I be able to stay ahead of it? What would my journey across the Mackinac Bridge be like? I wanted to get back to David's home as soon as I could to spend the rest of the weekend with the family. I hurriedly finished my breakfast, battened down the hatches, and said my good-byes to Bobbie and Dutch.

As I traveled southeast toward Mackinac Bridge, I reflected on all the beauty that I had experienced the last few days and asked God to please give me a safe trip back. A few light snowflakes began to dot my windows and the wind was starting to pick up. If it's too windy, they close the bridge. Because it is such a large suspension bridge, they are very cautious, especially on windy days. They insist that all the large trucks, motor homes, boats, and trailers caravan over the bridge following a pilot car. I could have opted to have someone else drive my vehicle, but I wasn't worried as I knew I would be driving slowly in the right-hand lane. All set in my caravan, I cautiously started to drive over the bridge.

So far, so good...oops, that wind is pretty strong!

Almost to the halfway point...

Just as I was driving past one of the large towers that support the bridge, a gust of wind slammed into my vehicle. Instantly, I heard grinding metal and then loud bangs, one after the other. Three screws that held each of the awning support bars in place had been ripped from the side of the motor home, leaving jagged, gaping holes. Gripping the steering wheel as I fought the wind to stay steady, I glanced at the right-side mirror and was alarmed to see the bars swinging way out and back the other way, hitting the rig with terrifying pressure. To make matters worse (and scarier), the railing of the bridge wasn't far away, so I tried to stay as close to the lane line on the left as I could. The next thing I knew, the awning bar swayed out so far and so high that it folded over and landed on top of the RV!

As I watched the remaining bar do its own little dance in the wind, all I could do was keep driving and frantically praying for God to keep me safe. It was a VERY long bridge and it seemed to take *forever* to get to the other side.

I took the first exit and pulled into a gas station and convenience store. I asked where the closest RV repair shop was and hoped and prayed that they would be open on a Saturday afternoon. They informed me that it was forty miles down the road. I explained my predicament and said I would not be able to drive until I was able to secure the two bars. They pointed out a car repair garage that was only two blocks away and said they might be able to help. I slowly and carefully drove the two blocks. As I pulled in, I noticed the name painted in large letters above the shop doors. I had arrived at "Krueger's Garage"! The large bay door was open, and two men were standing inside. I got out, walked into the shop, and asked if one of them was Mr. Krueger.

"We both are," one of them said. "He's my son."

"Well, I'm Mrs. Krueger and I need help!"

They quickly assessed the problem and got a ladder so they could bend back the front awning bar. I had some bungee cords, and they supplied a couple more so both the bars could be secured to the rig. It was a temporary fix, but it would get me back to my son's home.

I did enjoy and appreciate the beauties of a Michigan fall but what I delighted in the most was spending quality time with family. We went camping, took trips to town for ice cream, and played lots of cards. David and Cammie were looking for a larger home because of their expanding family. During my time there, I was able to share their joy when they found a beautiful, large country home on ten acres, with pastureland that would accommodate the children's 4-H livestock. As much as I hated to leave them, the shorter days and colder nights meant that I needed to start heading south. I had some new adventures waiting for me and always in the back of my mind was the question: *Will I find the new direction for my life on this leg of my journey?*

Favorite thing to do with my wonderful grandchildren:

Play Hand and Foot

My Spiritual Journey

As I was driving through some of the states, there would be hills to climb and then maybe a lovely, relaxing valley with a meadow of wildflowers.

Thank you, God, for Your beautiful world!

On the farm, even though we went through our hard times, we also had some enjoyable memories. I loved being a mom and enjoyed doing things with my children. I enjoyed being a mom so much that I became Mom to other couples, like Rick and Elva McNurlin and Brett and Shannon Morris. Both couples, their children, and grandchildren are still an important part of my life today.

During the time when we had to quit farming and start a new business, our two oldest were in college. We were not able to give any money toward their college education. Julie had been awarded the State of Idaho Scholarship, which paid most of her expenses. David had earned money from farming and some cattle he owned, which paid for the first two years. Our 1099 tax information was a big help because we were not making much money, so they were able to get a few grants and loans. My friend, Clarrisa Brown, was talking to someone who didn't know how their children would be able to go to college and she said, "If the Krueger kids were able to acquire a college education, anyone can do it."

Karma, our youngest, was still in high school, and active in 4-H. Her first love was her horses: Nugget, her palomino mare, was her favorite. She participated in horse shows continually, and the smile on her face when she brought home trophies and ribbons was worth the time we spent. She was very fortunate to win a two-year-old quarter horse from the State Quarter Horse Association the summer before her junior year and spent hours training "La La Love" so she could show her in 4-H.

We all enjoyed the occasional times we could get away in our small camper and park by a peaceful lake. There we would try to entice beautiful rainbow trout to bite. I loved the feeling of reeling in a nice sized trout, but I also enjoyed the ambiance of having a book in hand, listening to the water gently hitting the shoreline and the sound of birds enjoying their day. In the fall, we climbed into our four-wheel Ford pick-up, with the camper trailer behind, and drove into the majestic Idaho mountains to hunt deer and elk that would be our winter meat supply.

Julie graduated with a bachelor's degree in electrical engineering from the University of Idaho in May of 1984, then took a job as a product engineer for Intel in Chandler, Arizona. We had decided that I would drive down with her and look for an apartment and help her get settled in. We took our time stopping at Bryce Canyon National Park, Zion National Park, and even went on a boat trip on Lake Powell. We thoroughly enjoyed all the beautiful scenery and the fun of just traveling together. It was very hard for me to get on the plane and think about going back to mowing lawns and all the work that was waiting for me.

The next year David graduated from the University of Idaho, with a bachelor's in agriculture and extension education. We were part of a wonderful wedding the next day when David took Debbie to be his wife. They had been engaged for almost a year and we were happy to have this beautiful, talented young woman as part of our family. David and Debbie wanted to share the Kimberly reception with us as it was our twenty-fifth wedding anniversary. Debbie insisted that I wear my wedding dress, too. I know you might be wondering how I could still fit into my wedding dress. My main job was walking most of the day mowing lawns, and that is an excellent way to stay trim! The reception table held two beautiful cakes. One accented with apricot frosting, our wedding colors, and the other lavender, which was their wedding color. They would be living close to us as David had an agriculture teaching job at Buhl, Idaho. We were also blessed with another wedding. The young man that was like a son, Rick McNurlin, married Elva in August.

After all the happy events, another storm was about to hit our home life in Idaho, but this time, I didn't see the dark clouds gathering. I was utterly unprepared to receive the news that came, which would leave gaping holes in my heart that would take a very long time to heal.

I had our three children fairly young. Gene and I did the best we could to be good parents, but children don't come with instruction manuals when they are born. We taught them good values, to be well-mannered, to respect their elders, to have a good work ethic, and we gave them lots of love. They had their share of accidents, but most things could be handled with Aloe Vera and a band-aid. What we weren't able to keep them from were the emotional hurts. We weren't doing a very good job dealing with our own emotional scars, much less trying to observe the unseen wounds our children might have had.

The summer of 1989 was busy. Gene and his employee, Chris, were mowing lawns, and I was delivering mail full-time. Karma had graduated high school and was living out of town. I was busily trying to get our home cleaned and fixed up because we had decided to sell it and buy a smaller place, since all our children were out of the house. I was looking forward to the 4th of July weekend because Julie was coming from Colorado, where she had a good job and was doing well in her career. I always looked forward to having all my children home. We spent the weekend cooking, eating, playing cards and visiting.

One evening, when the whole family was gathered around, Julie said she had some important news to share with us. Was it a new job or maybe a new location? My mind was imagining all kinds of marvelous things when she dropped the bomb. As the fireworks were going off outside, I was inside trying to process what Julie was saying.

"I'm a lesbian and I discovered this a couple of years ago."

"I really believe this is how God made me."

"The reason for this trip is for me to come out of the closet."

"I have books and cassette tapes to leave with you, and when you study these, I am sure you will understand why I believe that this is the life that God has for me."

While she was saying this, fireworks were going off in my mind and I was thinking:

No, this can't be true.

NO, NO, NO!!!

Didn't I raise her in the church? She asked Jesus into her life at the age of eight.

She has read the Bible. Doesn't she know what it says about this?

She dated boys in high school.

Where did I go wrong?

These thoughts and many more were skyrocketing through my mind as I quietly looked at her. As the fireworks quieted down outside, the silence penetrated our living room as we were all trying to process what Julie had said. It took a while to get our voices back. Gene broke the silence and said, "if you are happy, I am happy for you." Just as that wind violently pulled the screws out of the motor home that Saturday in Michigan, leaving ragged, gaping holes, this news went into my heart like an arrow and as it was slowly being pulled out it left a bleeding, gaping hole in my heart.

While Gene and I were still trying to absorb the news that Julie had given us, we continued getting our home ready to sell. Just a few days after listing our home on August 8^{th,} we had a visit from Karma and her boyfriend, Jim Hamilton.

What now?

By this time, I was leery of any news our daughters might have for us. I didn't have to wait too long as Karma explained that she was pregnant, and they had decided the best option would be to get married as soon as possible.

Wow!!!

There went another arrow that was to leave another hole in my heart. I came from the era where you didn't live together before marriage and if you did get pregnant out of wedlock, it was a disgrace. It was usually a big family secret and some families even moved if their daughter became pregnant, or she was sent away. I wasn't very happy about this news, but at this point, not much could be done, so the question became, "When, where, and what needed to be done first?"

We decided to have the wedding in our back yard in six weeks. Planning a wedding in such a short time was a big task, but I had another concern that kept drifting through my mind. Karma had been diagnosed with juvenile diabetes when she was nine. I knew that, when an insulin-dependent diabetic woman becomes pregnant, there were many complications that could happen, both for the mother and the baby. All I could do at this point was to try and place all my worries and cares into God's hands.

It was just a year later when the third arrow hit. This time it came from David. In July of that year, he went to the University of Idaho for a four-week class that was required to finish his master's degree. He was pleased that he was able to finish the class ahead of schedule so looked forward to surprising his wife with an early return.

David was the one who was surprised because as he entered the front door, there was a big bouquet of flowers on the table that he knew was not from him. Debbie had met a man on one of her work trips and she made the decision to leave David. Satan loves to destroy marriages and he knows what kind of apple to use to tempt people. They had been active in church, participated in a small group, and we thought their marriage was great. This sad news was hard to process. These are the deep hurts that you can't fix with a band-aid. When your children are going through pain, you hurt right along with them.

"The LORD is near to the brokenhearted and saves those who are crushed in spirit."

Psalm 34:18

When the screws were pulled away from the motor home and left the gaping holes, that was just the beginning of the problems. I had the awning arms swaying back and forth, and then had to get the motor home safely to the end of the bridge. I needed help in securing them so I could finish that day's drive and then I had to make arrangements to get them permanently fixed.

This was also true after the heart-wrenching news we received that year. Between working full-time, trying to get the house ready to sell, and planning a wedding, I didn't have much time to study the material that Julie had left. I listened to some of the cassettes, glanced at the material, and we had some serious counseling sessions with our pastor, Jim Evans. Sometimes, I felt like I was on a big roller coaster, as my emotions went up and down. There was hurt, disappointment, sadness, grief, and pain. Then there were the constant questions going through my mind.

Was this my fault?

What should I have done differently?

What would people say if they found out? (This was almost thirty years ago, so that lifestyle wasn't very acceptable.)

I had a good firm foundation because I had been reading and studying the Bible faithfully for the previous twenty years. I believe the Bible is the inspired Word of God. So, what it says in Genesis 1:27, "So God Created man in His own image, in the image of God

He Created him male and female He created them" seems pretty clear to me, so it was hard to understand Julie's reasoning.

My motor home was completely fixed within a week, but the scars in my heart took much longer. The choices on my trip, like what road to take and should I veer to the left or go straight ahead were easy compared to the difficult choices Gene and I had ahead of us after our children shared their trials. There were many decisions to be made. The year Julie broke the news to us, she met someone that she wanted to be with for the rest of her life. Julie and Linda were planning on having a commitment ceremony on November 23, 1990, at Metropolitan Church, which was where they attended services in Colorado Springs. The question was, since I didn't really agree with that lifestyle, should we go to the ceremony? Julie said she would like us to attend, but she didn't want us to rain on her parade. There was an enormous amount of discussion and prayer that went into this decision. In November, as we were packing the pick-up for the long trip to Colorado, my heart was heavy and somewhat reluctant, but when our children were growing up, we said we would always be there for them. I can honestly say that being a mom to Julie through that process was one of the hardest things I have ever done. They did get legally married in Toronto, Canada, in July 2004. I try to follow Jesus in every area of my life and Jesus loves us with unconditional love, so shouldn't I give that same kind of love to my children? Over the past twenty-nine years, I have appreciated the help Julie and Linda have given me through the years. Julie and I both know that there are some things we don't agree on, but we still love each other.

The fall after Karma and Jim were married brought many questions and more choices to make.

When will our house sell?

When it does sell, where do we move?

There was also the question of Karma's health and concern that she would be able to deliver a normal, healthy baby. The month of December in the life of a rural carrier is the busiest, craziest month of the year. It was during the first week of this unbelievable work schedule that a family looked at our house. I sometimes wonder about God's timing. We were very thankful that they wanted to buy our home. Since their children were still at home and our children had left, they were wondering if we would be willing to exchange our bigger two-story for their smaller home built on one level. Another big plus was that they lived on my mail route. Two answers down, two (Karma and the baby) to go.

Even with all the things that were consuming my time, my thoughts were continually on Karma. She was going to a family doctor in the small community of Hailey who did not have a lot of experience with diabetic pregnancies. So, the best thing I could do was to leave the whole situation in God's capable hands.

That December was definitely an endurance race with the long workdays and packing up the house in my spare time, then sliding quickly into January, when we closed on the house. I didn't even have all the boxes unpacked at the new place when I flew to England in February to help Shannon Morris, who was like a third daughter to me, have her second child. While she and Brett were living in the Twin Falls area, Shannon's mother passed away, so I became her substitute mom. I had been there a week when baby Catherine Morris decided to finally enter the world on February 23. I stayed and helped for a week but was anxious to get back because Karma was due to deliver her baby shortly. Five days after my return, we got a call that Karma's doctor was concerned about the condition of the baby and wanted to do a cesarean delivery as quickly as possible. Before we could drive the seventy-five miles to the hospital, Skyler Hamilton was brought into this world on March 6th. I was thrilled and thankful that my first grandson was healthy, but this would be only the beginning of many challenging times ahead.

Just like I kept seeing the awning bars whipping in the wind and experiencing the fear of not knowing what was going to happen, I was experiencing the same feeling with Karma.

She followed through with her desire to complete her education while raising an active toddler. Finally, she received her nursing degree and entered the profession she loved. The joy of obtaining that goal soon was shadowed by the realization that her marriage was not going to work out. That led to the new trials for her of working and being a single mom.

We were also concerned about David as he was trying to make a new life for himself. As he prayed about what his next step should be, he decided it would be a good time to continue his education and get his Ph.D. He finally made the decision to go to Michigan State University. In the spring of 1991, he moved in with us after selling his home so he could save money for school. That summer he packed all his belongings into his pickup and headed for a new start in Michigan. I was excited for him, but we would sure miss him.

The combination of all these things left scars in my heart. The motor home was fixed with a new awning and added support plates for the awning bars. It looked like it never ever happened. No one would have ever imagined that I had the deep wounds in my heart that I did. I still functioned, helped at church, and worked my mail route. But complete healing took time and was a process. Reading the Bible, guidance from the Holy Spirit, and counseling were all helpful. The last few years I have read and listened to training from Katie Souza on soul healing. I also have taken three classes focusing on the healing of trauma and emotional wounds. All of that was very helpful, but it wasn't until April of 2017, at a meeting at my church, during worship, I saw Jesus take his hand, cover my heart and completely heal the scars that had been there.

There is nothing like the touch of Jesus' hand.

Emma, Alexis, and Matthew having special time with Grandma.

Me with my three children in Michigan.
From L – Julie, Donna, Karma, David.

Come to Me,
all you who labor and
are heavy laden, and
I will give you rest.

Matthew 11:28

Chapter Six

The Road of Refreshment

I'd like to dedicate this chapter to my dear friend, Nancy Goodwin, who is finding eternal rest and refreshment in heaven since her passing in December of 2018. She was an avid reader and would have loved being a part of my book.

As the sun glistened across the autumn leaves that covered the ground that Monday morning, November 1st, I hopped up into the driver's seat ready to head south. I turned on my music and reflected on the wonderful memories I had made in Michigan and wondered what God had for me on this leg of my journey. I was leaving the love and security of my family, but I was also looking forward to spending time with good friends.

The road into Indiana wasn't new to me because I had just traveled this highway three weeks earlier. My destination that beautiful fall morning was Warsaw, Indiana, where my Idaho friend, Sharon Harshman, was visiting her son, Brian, and his wife.

We spent a wonderful afternoon and evening catching up on everything, especially my trip and adventures on the Upper Peninsula because it was Sharon's mother and stepfather whom I had visited. The time together went way too fast; I was enjoying our visit so much that it was hard to pull myself away for the good night of sleep I desperately needed.

I lingered over breakfast with the Harshmans, and I enjoyed a second cup of coffee because this was going to be a short day of travel. Early that morning after studying the map, I implanted in my mind what roads I would be traveling. After pulling myself away from the company of good friends, I hopped back into the cab and took off for the day's drive.

After navigating around the city of Fort Wayne, Indiana, I relaxed and enjoyed my special praise and worship time with God and the leisurely three-hour drive to Leipsic, Ohio. As I got closer, my thoughts went to Roy and Nancy Goodwin, the couple I was going to visit. Roy became a special friend of my husband's during the late '50s when they were serving in the Army. We had kept in touch with them and had brought our family for a visit during a big Christmas marathon vacation. After we started farming and had just bought our new Ford pick-up in the fall of 1975, we decided we wanted to do a BIG Christmas vacation. We celebrated the holiday in Nebraska with Gene's parents, New Year's Eve with the Goodwin's in Ohio, then on to Texas to visit my sister and family. We were there for Karma's seventh birthday, January 3rd, and then back through Las Vegas so the children could get back to school. Crazy, but fun!!!!

At one point in the drive that day, I was going through a small town in Ohio. There was a section that had multiple highway signs all shouting different instructions. It was hard to try to stay on the correct road. I made it through the maze and was busy congratulating myself when I realized that, despite my very best efforts, I was on the wrong road!

I had to backtrack and was glad that I had studied the map before starting to drive that morning because I was able to catch my mistake fairly quickly.

When I was pulling in to the Goodwin's driveway, I noticed the large shop they had and remembered that Roy is a good mechanic. My motor home could certainly benefit from a knowledgeable man checking it over. While we were visiting, I asked Roy if he would be willing to change the oil, check the fluids, and give the whole rig a check-up. The next morning, after he spent several hours working on it, he came into the kitchen where Nancy and I were enjoying our visit.

"When was the last time you checked the oil?" he said soberly, making direct eye contact with me. "Do you have any idea how little oil was left in the engine?"

I knew that if Gene had been alive, he would be giving me the same lecture. I really knew better. Gene had always been a real stickler about reminding the kids and me to check the oil in our vehicles. I had been on the road for six weeks, but with the big accident, the slashed tire in Colorado, then getting the wind damage from crossing the Mackinac Bridge fixed, the thought hadn't even crossed my mind. I had ne-glected the everyday maintenance of my motor home. While we were out-side going over the dif-ferent things he had found  wrong, Roy also pointed to the inside dual tire on the right.

It was flat.

I immediately called Good Sam Roadside Service because changing a tire on a motor home is much harder than changing one on a car. I was very thankful that I had a good spare tire because it was put back into service until I could find the next Big O Tire Center. If my RV could talk, I'm sure he would say how much better he felt with clean oil in the engine, a few minor things repaired, and a good tire. I had enjoyed the extra day of rest and getting my spiritual tank filled through sharing how God had been working in each of our lives. Both the motor home and I were ready to leave the next morning refilled and refreshed.

My Spiritual Journey

Even with my busy, hectic life in Idaho, I tried to continue with the habit of getting up a little earlier so I could read and meditate on the Word of God and have a special quiet time with the Lord. I found that this was a great routine to have, especially when I was very busy. The rest of the day just seemed to go better, and I knew that no matter what, God was with me. It was during those times that the Holy Spirit would reveal the path that He had for me. I am human and there were times when I would get caught up in the cares of the world or my own selfish desires, and I would miss the road sign that God had posted. Just like when I got on the wrong highway in the small Ohio town, because I had studied the map, I knew I was on the wrong road and I corrected it quickly. The closer my relationship is with God, the more I am reading my Bible, the sooner I realize that I am on the wrong path and the quicker I turn around and get back on the road He has for my life.

"I'm single-minded in pursuit of You; don't let me miss the road signs you've posted."

Psalm 119:10 (The Message Bible)

There have been times in my life when I felt empty and drained; many of those times happened when I was trying to get through a major crisis or just trying to survive during the years of our life in Idaho. There was the big job of getting the crops in after Gene's heart attack. Then the years of hard work in hopes that we could continue farming. Another job was helping my children as they were going through difficult times of their own. Focusing on helping my husband start the lawn care business was another of those times. It was all these, plus more, that were a continual drain on my inner spirit. I was so busy trying to survive the major crisis that I wasn't taking care of myself and neglected my own daily maintenance.

As I have reflected on those years, I realize that during the major crisis that I was usually so busy that I was not spending time with God. I have been journaling since 1981, but during those trial-filled years when everything had fallen down and was suffocating me, I noticed the entries in my journal happened only once or twice every six months. I was running on empty most of those times. It was usually when I was at the bottom of the pit that I would reach out to God.

I discovered the best way to get spiritually filled up was to read and meditate on the Bible on a regular basis and listen to the Holy Spirit for guidance. During this special time with the Lord I would pray. I would not only talk to God about my prayer requests, but I took the time to spend time basking in His presence. I realized that the ultimate protection against sinking during the storms of life is devoting time to develop a special friendship with God.

Another way of getting filled up spiritually is praise and worship. Listening to and singing songs that bring God glory brings you into a closer bond with Him. I faithfully went to church, but I also connected with people outside of church. When I could, I would go to a Bible study or a prayer group. I found it was the prayers and encouragement of others that would carry me through the hard times.

"...not forsaking our own assembling together, as is the habit of some, but encouraging one another..."

Hebrews 10:25 (NASB)

In the last few years, I have learned some additional tools that I wished I had known then. I now pray and decree God's word.

"You will also decree a thing, and it will be established for you; so light will shine on your ways."

Job 22:28 (NASB)

The words we speak from the Bible have power and can potentially create life or death in our lives (James 3:5-10). There are many verses that tell us the importance of decreeing the Word. Author and speaker, Patricia King, has several good books on making decrees:

Decree, third edition

31 Decrees of Blessing

7 Decrees for 7 Days

(These and many other helpful resources can be found on Patricia's website, www. Patriciakingministries.com or on Amazon.)

Another exercise that I found helpful was to name my day. I learned this from the speaker and author Wendy K. Walters. I ask the Holy Spirit to help me find a name for my day. As an example, *"I name today ENCOURAGE. God, as you encourage me today, I will, in turn, look for others I can encourage."*

Learn to take authority over your day. I like to start out with:

"This is the day which the LORD has made; We will rejoice and be glad in it."

Psalm 118:24 (KJV)

You have a daily choice of how you are going to start the day. You can control the day or let the day control you.

Just as I took the time to refill and replenish the motor home and myself in Ohio, I found it was also important to take the time to refill and replenish my spiritual well-being. I was continually putting gas into the motor home and learned that putting God's word into my soul and applying it to my life needs to be a daily activity.

Roy and Nancy Goodwin

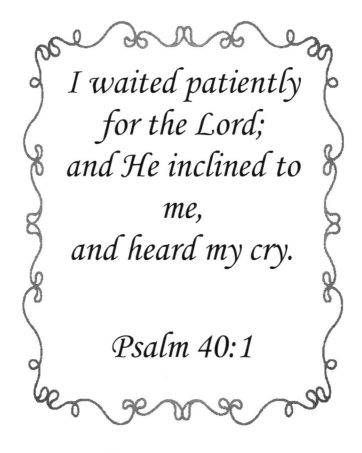

*I waited patiently
for the Lord;
and He inclined to
me,
and heard my cry.*

Psalm 40:1

Chapter Seven

The Valley of Difficult Choices

After spending some refreshing days with the Goodwins, I was ready to head south on my next adventure. I was enjoying the sun-brightened fall foliage and thinking about how it must have looked 150 years ago when my ancestors were living in this area of Ohio. My final destination that day was Wilmore, Kentucky, where my great niece, Tess Allen, lived with her husband, Paul, and their two boys. I was disappointed that I would not to get to see Tess and the boys, as they were enjoying a vacation with her parents in Texas. Paul encouraged me to come and take part in a Renovare Conference that was starting at 7:00 p.m. that evening, at Asbury Theological Seminary, where he attended.

I was again driving on the spare tire, so my next destination was the most convenient Big O Tire Store. Lexington, Kentucky became my first stop. I was thankful that this would be an easy driving day since Lexington was only four and a half hours away from the Goodwin's. I would have plenty of time to get my tire fixed, drive the forty miles to Wilmore, have dinner, and get ready for the 7:00 p.m. meeting.

That afternoon as they were putting a new tire on my rig, I sat with my well-used atlas, reviewing the options so I could memorize the best route to Wilmore. To be sure I was on the right track, I asked the cashier what road I should take, and he assured me that the highway we could see from the window was the correct one. Lexington is a large city and it was now mid-afternoon, so I thought it best to head out of the city and use country roads. After finishing up at the tire store, I confidently drove up the ramp to what the attendant had assured me was the correct road. It only took about ten minutes to discover I was on the right road…but going in the wrong direction. At the next exit, I corrected my mistake and backtracked. I finally got to the Blue Grass Parkway exit and immediately started looking for the highway I wanted. The next thing I knew, I was fast approaching an exit with multiple highway numbers listed; all but the one I wanted. With no time to decide (remember, no GPS), I just continued down the highway. Because of my earlier study of the maps, I knew that I could take a back way to their house, and I was now committed to going that route. By this time, I was very tired and wasn't making the best choices.

When I finally got off the Parkway and through a couple of small towns, the time was quickly slipping by. When I got on the right road it was starting to get dark, but I did pass a sign that said fifteen miles to Wilmore, so I knew my destination was ahead. What I didn't realize was what kind of road that fifteen miles was going to be. After a few miles of farmland, I found myself trying to maneuver a large motor home on a windy, narrow canyon road that had a cliff on one side and NO shoulder on either side. The white line was the edge of the road. I had to take curve after curve at fifteen mph and it seemed like it was going to go on forever. I was becoming very discouraged and kept wondering if I was ever going to get there. I was so relieved when the town finally came into view! I finally arrived at the Allen home and Paul met me at the door. After telling him about my round-about route, he exclaimed, "Oh, you took the scenic way!"

My life on the farm felt the same way as my drive into Wilmore did. I was taking a harder route because I was blinded by all the darkness around me. I hadn't been experiencing the light that God wanted me to travel in. As I look back on my life, there would have been several times when I could have chosen much better roads to take, but when I was in the midst of living, I made quick decisions and sometimes forgot to ask God for the best path. I often missed the correct "exit." I made choices that weren't the best for me or our marriage.

I am a person who likes to go all out and help others as much as I can. There have been times where I have helped too much, and it has not been good for them or me. That was the case after Gene and I quit farming and went looking for our next source of income. As I look back, I could have made better choices, but I missed the turn and ended up caught on the longer, more difficult path.

In the spring of 1984, we started our lawn care business. It was hard to start a new venture and, even after buying the equipment, hiring someone to help, and establishing customers, our hard summer of work hadn't left us with enough money to get through the winter. We bought a small snow blower, hoping to use it for extra income, but it ended up being a mild winter with not much snow. I had started working as a substitute mail carrier in Kimberly, however, it was a small route and I only worked when the regular carrier was sick or on vacation. Gene had been working two days a week at the livestock sale yard, so I started working there, too, pushing cattle through the maze of pens, in all kinds of hot and very cold weather, herding them into the sale ring. We each earned $25 a day, no matter how long the day was, and we were thankful for that. Still, there wasn't much food to be found when we looked into our freezer, refrigerator, or cupboards. One Sunday afternoon, Brett and Shannon Morris, whom we had recently welcomed into our family, came through our back door carrying sacks from the grocery store. They had just moved to our area after graduating from college, so buying all that food for us was a big sacrifice for them. A couple of months later, God blessed us with some food money from Julie and David's college youth group. As I reflect on that winter, the only way we got through was by the grace of God.

The next summer, our son, David, had a couple of college friends who needed work, so he talked us into running two crews. Rick McNurlin, whom we trusted, was willing to manage the second crew. We acquired more equipment and extra lawns to mow and we did bring in more money, but with all our extra expenses and labor, we still did not end up with much by the end of the summer.

After learning the hard way, during the summer of 1986, we settled into a much more doable work arrangement. God graciously blessed us with Chris, an efficient, hard-working woman, and she was a big help to Gene and me. As the morning sun rose each day, the three of us loaded up the equipment and prepared for a long day of mowing lawns.

Each day as I pushed a lawn mower back and forth over the lawns, I had plenty of time to think. What was my real destination? Was it just going back and forth in life? This certainly wasn't my dream. It was hard, physical work, but it was the working environment that caused me to be so exhausted as I trudged home each night. My husband was a negative, criticizing, fault-finding person. If anything went wrong, I was blamed for it. I was put down, made to feel unworthy, and I had been trained over the years of our marriage to do only as I was told. The daily verbal abuse made me feel hopeless, discouraged and worthless. I had lived with this for twenty-six years, but it was just during the last four when we worked closely together that it became more than I could handle. I was living in a very controlling atmosphere. I felt like a beautiful rosebud that was surrounded by large hands such that the rosebud was so completely enclosed that it didn't have a chance to bloom and become the exquisite flower that God had intended. I knew I was suffocating and slowing withering away in this environment but didn't know how to break out.

As I was journeying through this difficult time in life, I cried out to God and in desperation asked, "Where are You?" I felt like David when he exclaimed to God:

> *"Hasten to deliver me; O LORD, hasten to my help!"*
>
> *Psalm 70:1 (NASB)*

I knew that God had my hand and He would help me to find the way out, even if it didn't feel like it sometimes.

> *"I will strengthen you, yes, I will help you, I will uphold you with my righteous right hand."*
>
> *Isaiah 41:10 c, d*

I had to get to rock bottom, as they say, and stop struggling on my own. I had to turn the whole situation over to God.

I was finally able to say, "I surrender everything to You because I don't know what to do." I had reached the breaking point. I needed help from God to climb out of the deep hole I was in.

With the Holy Spirit's divine guidance, I knew that the first thing I had to do was explain to my husband that I was not going to work for him anymore. That fall, after the lawn season was over, that is exactly what I did.

Well, that went over like a lead balloon.

He didn't understand because, from his viewpoint, there was no problem. I often wish that we had learned to communicate better. I highly recommend marriage counseling, because we had both come from dysfunctional homes and had brought lots of baggage with us. I am sure some good Christian counseling would have helped.

The second thing I did was to go to town and look for a job because we needed the extra money. I had gotten married right out of high school and the only thing I had done besides working on the farm was selling Fuller Brush door-to-door (yes, I was a Fuller Brush lady!) After searching the help-wanted ads, I managed to acquire a part-time job selling advertisements for the *Eye Opener*, a printed flyer with jokes and stories, placed in restaurants to help people pass time while waiting for their food.

Gene wasn't happy with me going to town to work, but he finally came to the realization that I was not coming back to mow lawns with him. Gene still had Chris, who had worked diligently for us the last two years.

The third thing I did was look for a good Christian counselor. I had many soul wounds, which are hurts or trauma that were either so horrendous or have become so deeply rooted in a person that they have affected the core of their being. I needed a professional to help me through the healing process. Someone referred me to Susan Westendorf, who was a counselor at the Center for New Direction at our local junior college. She helped me to begin the process of healing. Also, since I was searching for the new path that God had for me, she encouraged me to take a couple of spring classes that were just beginning at CSI. Since our income was still very low, my oldest brother, Pat, agreed to pay for the fees.

What about my spiritual growth during this time? I had been in a valley for a long time and now I was slowly working my way, back and forth on the switchback trail, climbing up the large hill to get to a satisfying life.

> *"For momentary, light affliction is producing for us an eternal weight of glory far beyond all comparison."*
>
> *2 Corinthians 4:17 (NASB)*

When going through difficult times, it seems so much longer than a moment; it seems like it will never end. I also questioned where it said "light" affliction, because it didn't feel light to me. That challenging road in Kentucky probably wouldn't be nearly as difficult today in a car, in the daylight; but that evening, it seemed like it would never end. My home and work life seemed to be an impossible situation as I was going through it, with no light at the end of the tunnel. As I look back on that summer, I see that Jesus was with me, guiding and directing each step.

> *"Don't worry that you're not strong enough before you begin. It is in the journey that God makes you strong."*
>
> *Pass it On© Message Card*
> *Universal Designs*

The lesson I learned while going through each of these adventures is that God is going through those trying times right beside you. He does hear your cry for help and is waiting for you to turn everything over to Him.

> *"He will not leave you, nor forsake you."*
>
> *Deuteronomy 31:6c*

We have to remember that there is rarely an instant fix to our problems. There were times that I would have loved to have a helicopter swoop down, pick me up, and plop me onto an island paradise somewhere. That just doesn't happen. Sometimes you need to get professional help like I did. Getting through our hardships is a process and it goes back to spending time with God, reading the Bible, and praying. It is so important to spend a lot of time praising and thanking God, no matter the situation. The more you give Him thanks, regardless of your feelings, He will give you joy no matter what the circumstances. I had to learn to depend on Him daily. As I look back, I can see how much I grew spiritually when going through the trials.

> *"Count it all joy when you fall into various trials, knowing that the testing of your faith produces patience. But let patience have its perfect work, that you may be perfect and complete, lacking nothing."*
>
> *James 1:2-4*

Our wedding portrait and a picture of us, still together, after many years of the ups and downs of life.

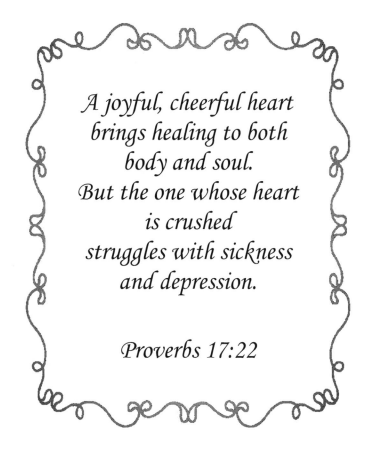

A joyful, cheerful heart
brings healing to both
body and soul.
But the one whose heart
is crushed
struggles with sickness
and depression.

Proverbs 17:22

Chapter Eight

Making Time for Fun Detours

It was a crisp, sunny November morning, and I was focused on maneuvering along the busy Tennessee freeway. The music was saturating the atmosphere of my Jayco motor home, and I was enjoying the colorful fall leaves, trees, and gorgeous flowers. I traveled from the Allen's home in Wilmore, Kentucky, to visit my good friends, the Bardill's, in Sanford, North Carolina. Betty and Curly had been our best friends in Idaho, and I was anticipating a wonderful visit with them. On this trip, my focus had been to visit friends and family, so I would often go from one destination to the next with no sightseeing in between. I was sure I could do this drive in one day.

After enjoying the morning drive, I stopped for lunch. As I was eating my green salad and turkey sandwich, I gazed out the window and noticed the extreme amount of traffic on the roads. My phone rang, interrupting my thoughts. It was David, checking in to see how I was doing. I commented about the traffic and was wondering if there was some big event going on that I was missing. He wanted to know where I was, and I explained that I was next to Hwy 66, which went to Servierville.

"I know just where you are! You're on the road to Pigeon Forge, the home of Dolly Parton's Dollywood, and not far from Gatlinburg."

He encouraged me to take the extra time to detour and see those special attractions. Before going on, I called my friends and said I wouldn't be there until the next day, then I crowded my way into the lineup of traffic heading south.

 I knew I was going to have fun as soon as I stepped out of my motor home into the magical land of Dollywood and heard the music and saw all the lights. The whole place was decorated for Christmas, which I love, so I was able to watch a special show and enjoy all the beautiful decorations. I had never experienced such a wonderful place. I walked around the park for hours, immersing myself in the beautifully lighted trees, the stores full of gorgeous dolls and toys, and the other fabulous decorations, as Christmas music filled the air. I stopped to have some ice cream after watching the amazing holiday show. I was enjoying my treat at an outside table, where I visited with the couple beside me. They encouraged me to also see the Biltmore estate near Asheville, North Carolina. They insisted it was a must-see and that it was on my way. I looked at my watch and the fast-setting sun and knew I needed to get on the road, but I felt like a child being pulled away from the candy store. I didn't have a plan yet for staying the night but wanted to get further along before finding a camp ground.

My Spiritual Journey

Gene and I had some fun detours in our busy life. Wintertime in the life of farmers was more relaxing and we enjoyed playing cards with family and friends. We had taken several wonderful trips, but I think the best one was when we went to Alaska in August of 2000. Julie and Linda gave us this trip for our fortieth wedding anniversary, and we enjoyed traveling and celebrating with them. There were so many blessings, like Julie upgrading us to first class so Gene and I could sit side-by-side in the plane, holding hands while enjoying the sunset go on forever and ever as we traveled north. We stayed Saturday night with our friend, Priscilla, in Anchorage, and the next day we picked up our small rented motor home and stocked it with what we would need for the week. Our plan was to do a week on land and the last week on a cruise ship.

I couldn't believe it was already Tuesday; so much had happened in the last twenty-four hours. Gene was driving and I was up front enjoying the fantastic Alaskan countryside on our way to Denali Park. The girls had fixed sandwiches for all of us after our morning visit to the Alaska State Fair. Our plan had been to see the fair Monday, but we had an unexpected detour.

I remember how the sun was shining so brightly on Monday afternoon. I had made arrangements with a flight company in

Talkeetna, Alaska, for a flight around Mountain McKinley, which included landing on a glacier. We had scheduled it for Tuesday afternoon, but the owner had said if it was a sunny day to call and reschedule because there were not that many clear days. When I had called to change the flight, he encouraged us to come right away.

Julie had a friend who lived Anchorage, so Julie and Linda were riding with her. After talking to Doug, we pulled over and discussed our options. We decided to park the motor home in Wasilla and ride with Julie's friend to Talkeetna. Little did we know what was just ahead for us…

Twenty-four hours later, as we rolled along on our way to the national park, we excitedly shared about all that happened the day before

Linda turned to Julie and said, "That was so nice of your friend to be willing to change her plans at the last minute."

Gene turned to me and commented, "That was smart of you to call Doug about our trip around Mount McKinley when you did."

"I think we were about halfway there when I saw that van coming right at us from the other side of the road," Julie added.

"Julie, your friend tried to avoid the accident, but just couldn't turn the wheel fast enough to the left," Gene noted.

I piped in with, "When I saw it, the two right wheels were off the ground as it was heading right toward us!"

Gene, who had been sitting in the front passenger seat when it happened, replied, "I could see the underside of the vehicle as it got close and then the bottom of the tire went right across the top of my window!"

"I bet the reason none of us got hurt was because it was balancing on two wheels so there wasn't the solid impact," Linda chimed in from the back.

Each of us had our own story about the long delay due to the accident, including the police and ambulance getting there and our concern about not being able to do our glacier flight.

I had left the guide's information in the motor home and had been upset about that. Julie laughingly said, "Mom, it was so funny when you went up to the ambulance and asked the lady if she had a phone book! She asked who you wanted to call and when you told her about our appointment with Doug Geeting, she reeled off his number without a second thought! It was so great of her to volunteer to call Doug and explain the situation."

"I'm so thankful for the long evenings that made it possible for us to fly around the mountain and land on the glacier," said Gene.

I commented, "I thought it was *awesome* to fly so close to the mountain and experience the marvelous view without having to actually climb it!"

Linda laughed. "It was so much fun making snow angels when we were on the glacier."

"It turned out to be such a fantastic day," I added. "I especially enjoyed the dinner served outside of that gorgeous lodge while we watched the sun slowly go down on the magnificent view of Mount McKinley. It was the perfect ending for such a crazy-wonderful day!"

I have discovered that I need to be open to detours that God might have for me as well. It might be a special, fun event or activity that He wants to bless me with. God also might put me on a detour because He has a person He wants me to bless. Some of the detours might have a big bump, like the accident in Alaska. God didn't want me to get stressed out and be overcome with worry and concern. I needed to trust God so thoroughly that I would be able to turn the situation over to God and praise Him for what He was going to do. None of us were hurt in the accident. God provided someone who could let the guide know our situation, and the two people in the other vehicle were shook up but had no serious injuries. We didn't let it ruin our day. It is possible to enjoy God and glorify Him in the midst of adverse circumstances. I have found that, more often than not, things don't go the way I have planned, but if I put my complete trust in God, I can still have peace knowing that He is in control. Adversity is not a detour; it is part of the path.

> *God's light shines most brightly through believers who trust Him in the dark.*
>
> *Adapted from Psalm 112:4 (NLT)*

This is a supernatural trust that comes from spending time with God and listening to the Holy Spirit's guidance. God is much less interested in everything going the way we planned than He is in us responding with thanksgiving and trust to whatever comes our way.

Too often, I know I let my mind fill up with negative thoughts that really are from Satan. I have a choice to not listen to the negative thinking or ungodly belief and instead learn to replace it with a truth from God's word. A good, Godly truth for that day was:

> *"And we know that all things work together for good to those who love God, to those who are the called according to His purpose."*
>
> *Romans 8:28*

I have been surprised often with my detours in life. They are some of my most precious memories. I joyously got behind the wheel after a marvelous detour afternoon in Dollywood. The darkness was settling in fast. Thinking back on my previous nighttime experiences, the best choice would have been for me to find the closest campground, but with my charging-ahead attitude, I decided I could drive for a little while so I would be closer to Ashville, North Carolina.

I had no idea what lay just ahead.

L-R: Julie, Donna, Gene, and Linda on a glacier in Alaska.

For God, who said, "Light shall shine out of darkness," is the One who has shone in our hearts to give the Light of the knowledge of the glory of God in the face of Christ.

2 Corinthians 4:6

Chapter Nine

The Way to the Light

By the time I got to Gatlinburg after my visit to Dollywood, it was dark. I was supposed to make the next left, but the turn lane was already full and it's not like I could just nudge my rig into the line of traffic, so I sailed right by. I continued up Main Street to turn around, but the quaint little town was *crawling* with tourists. There I was, all 27' of me, stopping constantly, worried every minute that I might miss someone darting across the street in the dark. I finally breathed a big sigh of relief once I made it to the other end, until I realized that I had to find a place to turn around and then do it all over again!

I finally got myself on the right road only to find that it was horrible; bumpy and full of construction signs and torn-up sections. I slowly negotiated my big rig along on this dark road. This area of the Smokey Mountains was scenic, or so I'd heard, since I couldn't see anything but a few yards of road in front of me. My mind flashed back to the campground sign I had passed forty minutes before. I had just wanted to get further along on my long drive, but now I was kicking myself for not stopping there for the night. I had never anticipated that the curvy mountain road to I-40 would be so torn up. By this time, I was weary and willing to stop at the first campground I saw, but the few I passed had big "CLOSED" signs dangling on posts. Discouragement and despair settled over me like a big dark cloud.

Why did I even decide to do this trip anyway?

What was I thinking! I'm a sixty-two-year-old single woman driving a motor home by myself across the country!

Why, oh, why didn't I stop at that campground???

In that moment, darkness wasn't just settling in for the night; it was overwhelming me emotionally. I began to remember other dark times I'd had on the farm when the work seemed like it was never going to end. Earlier in my trip, I had an accident because of unlit surroundings, so you would have thought I might have learned not to drive after dark.

Oh, well. I just have to press through until I get to the interstate and then, hopefully, I'll be able to find a place to camp.

Interstate 40 ahead!

My heart jumped when the motor home lights reflected on the sign that indicated that Interstate 40 was not far away. I breathed a sigh of relief when my tires began to roll on smooth paved road as I anticipated a much easier drive.

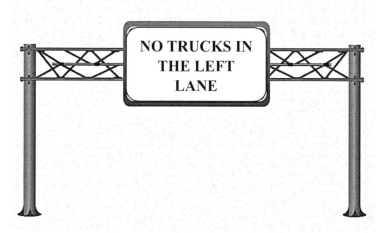

NO TRUCKS IN
THE LEFT
LANE

My joy was short-lived when I saw that sign. Glancing in my rear-view mirror, I saw the line of impatient semi-truck drivers who couldn't pass me. Just when I thought the journey might get better, the stress continued. I was *exhausted* from my extremely long day, guiding my RV slowly along the mountainous interstate, around curves that followed the Pigeon River, looking for a turnout where I could pull over to let everyone pass me. I finally did, but that forty-five miles of horrendous freeway traffic felt like it was 145 miles!

Help, Lord!

It was now after 9:30 p.m. and I desperately needed to find a place to stay. After stopping in a lighted parking lot in Canton, North Carolina, I pulled out my Passport America catalog and searched for the closest campground. I was so thankful when the owner answered the phone! I asked if he had a site I could stay in for the night, then he explained that, in early September, Hurricane Francis came through and then, less than two weeks later, Hurricane Ivan hit. Because of fifteen inches of rain, the Pigeon River had exceeded its sixteen-foot banks and his whole campground had been under water. They had been closed for weeks, repairing the underground wiring, and replacing electrical boxes. He could tell by my shaky, fearful voice how crucial it was for me to find a safe place to stay. They had not reopened since the flood, but he assured me that he had a unit I could stay in. Their information sign was still not working, so his wife, with a flashlight in hand, went to the road and guided me in. That light shining through the darkness brought me direction and hope.

As I sipped my mourning coffee I thought about the night before. It all started to make sense. I had followed the path where two hurricanes had preceded me so that explained the road construction and closed campgrounds. Because of Hurricane Ivan, Interstate 40 and the Pigeon River Gorge sustained major damage.

During my lifetime, God has put me through some major construction. Then there were the choices that my children and myself had made that made my road of life hard and difficult to navigate.

I am very thankful that Jesus has been my faithful shining light, always gently guiding me in the right direction. It seems in my deepest despair, God has always reached into my darkness and rescued me.

My mind flashed back to a very dark season in my life. I was caught up in an unpleasant journey, and just like I felt at that moment, I couldn't see the light at the end of the tunnel. I had found myself in a rut. I had been caught up in mowing lawns with my husband and at the time I could not see the end. I did make a quality decision to find a better path for my life. Getting professional help was the beginning of pulling more light into my dark world. Going back to school at forty-four was scary but at the same time exciting.

What classes should I take?

What was my new direction in life?

After discussing it with my counselor, I decided my main class would be in advertising, since that was the job I had at the time and selling things seemed to be easy for me. The second one was speech, which I thought would be an easy one since I have never had a problem talking.

Now, here I was sitting in class, surrounded by young students talking about the demographics of the audience we wanted to reach.

This is so much fun, and the professor is so amusing.

I DO have a brain and a certain amount of intelligence!

Here I am, learning a new skill and feeling better about myself!

I love expanding my mind and learning new things!

At the end of the semester, a local business came and interviewed a couple of us, and I ended up getting the job of selling advertisements for Moore Publishing Company. They were responsible for several local publications, like the yearly *Twin Falls Industrial Guide, Real Estate Today*, a monthly realtor magazine, and projects for the Idaho Travel Commission, like the *Burley Boat Regatta*. I even learned new things, like how to use a computer. Does anyone else remember using floppy discs and terminals that looked like boxes? It was a fun exciting job and I met many great people. Thankfully, the job was very versatile and, since I was working on commission, I was able to keep my part-time job at the post office.

Months later, I was extremely surprised when I received a call from the public service TV station in Boise, Idaho. They wanted to do a short documentary about a farm wife who was starting over after going broke on the farm. I agreed to be interviewed, so they spent most of a day filming the farm and my work and doing a nice interview in my home. In the film, Rita Laron, from the Center for New Directions said, "Donna has a lot of strength and a desire to do something different, and I know that maintaining a positive attitude has been a struggle for her." It was a struggle, but God was with me through it all. My strength during this time came from the LORD.

> *"God is our refuge and strength, a very present help in trouble."*
>
> *Psalm 46:1 (NKSV)*

In the fall of 1987, my youngest daughter, Karma, and I both attended classes at the College of Southern Idaho (CSI). I decided to take a class in marketing since I gained so much confidence in the advertising class. As much as I enjoyed the class, it was extremely stressful to work two jobs, go to school, and be a good wife and mother. This was one of the many times that I over-booked my time. When I do this, it is my time with God that suffers the most. It's when going through stressful times that we need God the most.

In January of the next year, I decided that it would be the best decision to stop my college career. I still had two jobs, but it was important to spend more time with family. Gene and I were getting along better, but Karma was making some bad choices that worried us. Karma was still living at home, but she was spending too much time having fun and neglecting her classes. She had been an A student in high school and now she was flunking out of an easy junior college. Just like on that Tennessee road, when I was thinking that if I got to the freeway, it would be better. I was thinking that if I was home more, it might be smoother. Well, it didn't happen that way. In trying to keep her connected with God and her faith, I said I would go with her to the church of her choice. I was praying that she would connect with a better group of friends. Looking back, I now realize that during her years in high school, I wasn't there enough because I was too busy trying to help my husband start a new business. That is when she really needed a mom and started going down the wrong track. I know it is important to be home for your children when they are little, but it is just as important to be there for them when they are teenagers. I was trying to be there for her now, but she was at a point where she would rather be with her friends.

The rough road we were going through now was caused by Karma's teenage rebellion and the only and best thing we could do in this storm was pray.

When I prayed for our family, children, or any situation, I found it is important to pray words of life. I didn't pray the problem because that empowers the problem. I didn't remind God of all the things that were wrong. He already knows all that. I prayed the Word of God into the person's life. This is an effective way to pray:

God, I thank You that You have a plan for Karma's life to give her a future and a hope (Jeremiah 29:11). I thank You that You said that all my children shall be taught by the LORD, and great shall be their peace (Isaiah 54:13). I know that You are always interceding for her and she is secure in Your hands. I pray that Your kingdom come, and Your will be done in Karma's life. That You will guide her on the path You have for her.

We create or destroy with the words we speak and pray. It is best to pray Scripture and pray words of life.

It wasn't easy for Gene and I when we were in the midst of raising a teenager who wanted to do her own thing. We had set some rules for living in our home. Karma wasn't obeying the rules, so there was a point where we had to practice tough love.

Karma ended up moving out and living with her boyfriend, and she often learned life lessons the hard way. She eventually survived this storm in her life and did come back to a closer relationship with God, but it took time and much prayer.

In June, I did finally get a full-time job with the Post Office. It was good to just have only one job and settle into more of a routine.

It is during some of our darkest times that the light of Jesus shines the brightest. He will continually and faithfully be there helping us, and our children, find His way.

The only dry spot in the entire campground after the hurricanes had gone through.

*Guide me down the
road of your com-
mandments;
I love traveling
this freeway!*

Psalm 119:35

Chapter Ten

Different Roads That Shaped My Journey

I was very tense and frustrated about being sandwiched between a truck and a car on the six-lane Interstate 285, as I skirted around the north side of Atlanta. It wasn't even 3:30 p.m. and my lane was not moving. I was mumbling to myself and God.

Why didn't I get on the road sooner?

What is causing such a standstill? It feels more like a parking lot than a freeway!

I had stayed the night before in Gainesville, Georgia, in a small Walmart parking lot in the middle of town. I wasn't very comfortable with the location, so I called my son before I went to sleep. I told him that if he didn't hear from me in the morning, he'd know where to start looking for me.

Oh, Lord, please send Your angels of protection for me tonight!

The reason I was staying in Gainesville was that it was where Crown Financial Ministries was then located. I had listened to Larry Burkett's radio program, *Money Matters,* while delivering mail for years. This was another ministry opportunity I wanted to check out. I had let them know I was coming, so they had a welcome sign out for me. After a tour of their facilities, they invited me to stay and listen as they recorded a radio program. I did want to get to Atlanta before rush hour traffic, but they assured me they would be starting the show soon. It all took longer than anticipated, so here I was stuck in bumper-to-bumper traffic.

Besides the obvious frustration, I could *hear* my rig slurping gas like it was cold lemonade on a hot day.

The car in front of me decided he'd had enough and was trying to get into the lane to our left.

Do I dare try to get into that lane? At least it's moving.

Would I be able to make it clear over to the right lane before my exit?

How far away was my exit anyway?

With that much traffic and my large vehicle, it wasn't going to be easy to switch lanes. I only was going to be on the I-285 for fifteen miles, but at this snail's pace it was taking f-o-r-e-v-e-r. Remember, no GPS to show me how much further I would have to go to get out of the traffic.

Maybe I had just better stay in this lane.

`This gave me plenty of time to think about the different roads I had traveled on over the course of my life. I loved the familiar rural Idaho roads that I had cut my teeth on. They are wide, paved roads with plenty of room on each side, and they are laid out in mile sections so are effortless to navigate. Instead of venturing into unknown territories, it would have been easy to stay in my little corner of the world where everything was familiar. But I knew I was at a crossroad in my life, and my decision was to expand my knowledge and explore what was outside my little bubble.

When I started my trip, I pictured myself steering my perfect little RV through a beautiful flower-filled meadow, following an easy flowing stream with sun beams dancing on the water. It never entered my mind there would be dark mountainous roads with many curves, continual construction, big city traffic, or traveling in wind, rain and even snow. During my trip I traveled a broad variety of roads which added up to a very interesting journey.

Leaving the busy interstate highway and venturing onto the slower more relaxing countryside roads were some of my most enjoyable times. The less-traveled roads that meandered through low hills or over a charming bridge with a view of the clear water below were my favorites. I loved slowing down to go through small towns with vintage buildings, and I often wondered what life was like for the people who lived there.

In life, I also enjoyed the times I was able to slow down and take a good look at how God was blessing me. In Attica, Indiana, after I  found the section of land where my great-great- grandparents lived 190 years ago, I took a little excursion to see the area where they had lived. As I drove around their land, I imagined I was driving the same route they had traveled, but on much improved roads, and it gave me a small connection with my heritage.

As I journeyed along the meandering narrow roads in the south, I was sure they had developed from well-worn trails that the original settlers had followed 300 years ago. I would be traveling through the beautiful countryside and come upon a charming little church and I imagined all the singing and preaching that had gone on in those four walls over the years. I loved the road in North Carolina because it took me to my long-time friends, the Bardills, in Sanford, North Carolina. The road to Raleigh, which I took to visit my great-nephew and family, ended up being the easternmost highway on my trip.

Now here I was trying to navigate around Atlanta to get to my friend Diane's home before dinner.

Is there ever a good time to go around Atlanta?

A blaring horn brought me back to this highway that I was *parked* on. The truck in front started to move and I crept along until I finally passed the accident that was holding up the traffic. I soon came to my exit and was thankful to find my friend's house in Marietta, Georgia, and unwind after a stressful afternoon of driving. Diane and I had gone to church together in Twin Falls, and it was one of those pleasant times of reconnecting with a good friend.

I left the next morning heading toward Alabama. One of the roads of life that I enjoyed very much was being a mom and grand-mother. Brett and Shannon Morris had been part of our family for twenty years and they were now living in Northport, Alabama. I was "Grammer" to their five children, so I was looking forward to some quality time of sowing into their lives. Their four girls, ages eight to fourteen, had American Girls dolls. I helped them plan a tea party with their friends and dolls. They all dressed in their fancy dresses and enjoyed sipping tea with their little pinky finger up. It was great spending Thanksgiving with "family."

The Sunday after Thanksgiving, I took a break from motor home life and boarded a train for New Orleans, Louisiana, where I met my brother Pat and his wife Elsa. We had scheduled a five-day riverboat adventure called *Music on the Mississippi*, which went from New Orleans to Memphis, Tennessee. While floating down the large

Mississippi river, I learned that it had been a highway for both the Native Americans and the early settlers and served as a very important thoroughfare.

After my river trip, I returned to the Morris home. I was able to spend ten days and have an early Christmas with them before flying back to Idaho for a month and spending Christmas with family and friends.

My Spiritual Journey

Just like I experienced a diversity of roads on my trip, I have also traveled different roads and have experienced many things in life. Some of the time the road was relaxing and fun and other times it was not. I had a variety of jobs and had many different titles.

Daughter (Baby of the Family)

Wife (Cook, Housekeeper, Companion)

Mom (Nurse, Teacher, Encourager, and Counselor)

Farm Wife (Gardener, Lawn Mower, Food Processor, Handyman, Parts Buyer, and Field Worker)

Friend (Listener, Encourager)

Just as I enjoyed driving the motor home through a beautiful scenic countryside, I also had some wonderful experiences in Idaho. We enjoyed picnics on warm summer evenings, camping in the mountains, or family nights of playing cards and games.

I was a 4-H mom for sixteen years, and I could write a whole book on all the interesting things I experienced. I learned to comb and back comb a cow's tail into a ball. I had the challenge of trying to get black shoe polish out of a white shirt just minutes before show time because Karma's horse rebelled over having its hooves painted.

One time, my youngest daughter, Karma, and I were on our way to a special 4-H meeting with her sheep and palomino mare in tow. Karma's show sheep was under the camper shell of the pick-up and her palomino mare was riding in our single-axle horse trailer. Suddenly, we heard and felt a big jolt, and when I glanced out my side window, I saw the wheel of the trailer rolling past us! I somehow managed to pull over to the side of the road and immediately hopped out and began to calm down the horse, the sheep, and my daughter before calling for help. We were delayed that busy day due to an errant trailer tire. I was delayed on my road trip by traffic and road construction. Sometimes it feels like things are delayed in our lives, or that God is taking too long to help us, but what we don't see is how God is working behind the scenes, putting something in place or slowly working in a loved one's life.

Because of my deep love for God and my eagerness to serve Him, I have been a part of various ministries. I love to share what God has done for me and to encourage others to come from a life of darkness and despair into the glorious light of Jesus Christ. I also have compassion for the hurting and wounded. In my desire to help, I have taught Sunday School and Bible studies. I was a leader with Christian Women's Luncheons, and Aglow International. I was a chaplain in the detention center and county jail. I've also held different offices in the church and have organized women's retreats. I led Grief/Share classes in both Idaho and in Arizona. I have always wanted to be available to whatever God wanted me to do.

In the fall of 1998, I thought I had a pretty busy life with working full-time on my mail route in addition to home and church responsibilities, but God had a new assignment for me. I had been praying the prayer of Jabez:

"O that you would bless me indeed and enlarge my territory, that Your hand would be with me, and that You would keep from evil, that I may not cause pain."

I Chronicles 4:9-10

I had been chaplain to the women in the Twin Falls County Jail for several years. We would share God's love, and many had asked Jesus into their lives. When they were released from jail we were not allowed to follow up or have any contact with them. Some of the women really had a desire to change, but it was so easy to go back to their old friends and habits. Several of us had talked about the need for an aftercare program, but nothing had been done. Soon after I had prayed the Jabez prayer, I heard that still small voice of the Holy Spirit saying, "Why don't you start an aftercare program?" Not sure where I would find the time or if I even had the knowledge, I dialogued back and forth with God to be sure that was what He wanted me to do. I asked for a sign that would confirm if this was truly from Him. The next Sunday when I was doing a Bible study with the ladies in jail, one of them expressed a desire to have help when she got out. I knew then that God wanted me to start this program.

I found out that the Prison Fellowship organization had a good aftercare program available. I flew to a conference in Southern California to receive training. I spent many hours recruiting mentors for both men and women from different churches in the area and then taught training classes. I found out that it was easier to get money for the program than it was getting people who would give their time. It was set up so if an inmate wanted a mentor, they would fill out a card. The selected mentor was allowed to talk with the inmate while they were still in jail, and there was a notebook to be filled out with their goals after they were released. The mentor then would meet with them regularly after they got released and hold them accountable to the goals they had set up. The aftercare program eventually grew larger and expanded to setting up homes for inmates when they were released. God just wants people who are willing and available, and He will be there with you through the process.

I was so busy with the "enlarging your territory" part of Jabez prayer that I hadn't given much thought to the "O, that You would bless me indeed" part. The next spring, when I attended my first Pregnancy Crisis Center banquet, I bought one raffle ticket to help with their program. I was utterly shocked when I was the top prize winner and utterly blessed with a six-person Jacuzzi spa! God knew how chilled-to-the-bone I was in the winter after working on my mail route, and He gave me a fantastic gift.

When I gave God total control of my life, I subconsciously thought that the road He would guide me on would be a much easier and enjoyable road without many bumps, steep inclines, or potholes. I guess I thought that it would be like gliding along a freeway or enjoying a mountain view as I meandered on a relaxing Sunday drive. However, it was more like being plopped in the middle of a jungle with a machete just trying to find the right path. In the last fifty years on the road of my life, I have experienced unexpected curves and dead-end roads. I've had to yield my right-of-way to others, and sometimes I had to stop completely, or proceed with caution. I always knew the one way, the right way, the best way: staying committed to God and His way. No matter how rough the road was, with His help, I always made it through. When I was on my road trip, there were so many construction signs that slowed me down or forced me to detour, but all of it was for the purpose of making a better, more durable road for all travelers. When God was doing construction on me, it sometimes felt like the work was going to go on forever. He was doing it so I would be a stronger, more durable women.

Me on the New Orleans waterfront.

That He would grant you, according to the riches of His glory, to be strengthened with might through His Spirit in the inner man, that Christ may dwell in your hearts through faith; that you, being rooted and grounded in love, may be able to comprehend with all the saints what is the width and length and depth and height— to know the love of Christ which passes knowledge; that you may be filled with all the fullness of God.

Ephesians 3:16-19

Chapter Eleven

The Vast Dimensions of God's Love

Look out, Texas—here I come!

I had taken a thirty-day break from the road trip, having flown back to Idaho to spend Christmas with family and friends. It was important to have a time of rest so I could come back refreshed with renewed energy. I had left my home-on-wheels in the care of the Morris family in Alabama and enjoyed a week with them before continuing with my quest to discover the place God had for me.

My motor home had rested in Alabama for over two months, so it was a great feeling to be behind the wheel again, just God and me, enjoying the clouds dancing through the blue skies. Mississippi and Louisiana were new states for me, so I was intently taking in the scenery and the different terrain. It didn't seem that long ago that I had cruised the massive Mississippi river, and now I had the joy of crossing over that beautiful body of water. I was well into Louisiana, enjoying the trees and the leisurely drive when suddenly the steering wheel was doing its own little dance and the motor home started to shudder.

Oh no, not another tire!

I had just passed a sign for a rest area, so I reacted quickly to maneuver into the right lane because the exit was rapidly approaching. It was times like this that I knew the angels were watching over me because the timing could not have been better!

Another flat tire.

Well, at least I have a good place to wait for Good Sam, the roadside service *to come.*

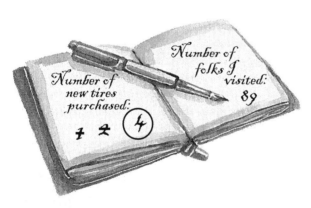

My faithful well-used spare tire took me to Shreveport, Louisiana, where I decided to buy two new tires. Since it was late in the after-noon, I found a place to stay the night and make my much-anticipated entrance into Texas after a good night's rest.

Why all the excitement about Texas? Well, it was the largest state I would be traveling through, but the main reason I was so elated was that some of my dearest family members live there, and I was so looking forward to spending time with them. My only sister, Bobbie, was married to a career Army man, Lee Keeney, who retired at Fort Hood in Killeen, Texas. My sister had passed away six years earlier, and her husband and four children still lived in Texas.

The vastness and diversity of Texas were evident in nearly all aspects of its physical features, economy, history, and cultural life. Because of all of this and more, it reminds me of one of my favorite Bible verses:

> *"I ask Him to strengthen you by His Spirit--- not a brute strength, but a glorious inner strength—that Christ will live in you as you open the door and invite Him in. And I ask him that with both feet planted firmly on love, you'll be able to take in with all followers of Jesus the extravagant dimensions of Christ's love. Reach out and experience the breadth! Test its Length! Plumb the depths! Rise to the heights! Live full lives fully in the fullness of God."*
>
> *Ephesians 3:16-19 (The Message Bible)*

Over the time I was in Texas, I experienced the breadth as I drove from east to west on my way in and out and the length as I visited family and friends up and down the state.

I arrived at Linda and Tim Floy's home in Grapevine, Texas, on the afternoon of January 25, 2005. Linda is my sister's oldest child. Bobbie was fourteen years older than I am, so her children are pretty close to my age. My nephew, Bob Keeney, and wife, Barb, also lived in Grapevine. Many years before, when Linda and Bob were teenagers, they each came out separately and spent the summer with us on the farm, so now it was payback time. The Floy's front driveway was long enough to accommodate my twenty-seven-foot rig so that became my home base.

As a child, I loved to play with my yo-yo. You all remember yo-yos, right? My stay in Texas reminded me of my yo-yo days because I kept going up and down the state for the next two months visiting with family and friends

135

While in Grapevine, I divided my time between Bob, Barb and the Floys. Bob was a pilot for American Airlines, and I went to their house on his days off. They owned their own sailboat, so I loved the days we went sailing around Grapevine Lake with the thrill of gliding through the water and the wind blowing through my hair. After Bob gave me a few instructions on sailing he said, "Here, take the wheel." With much trepidation and under his watchful eye, I guided the sailboat through the captivating water. With a twinkle in his eye, he grinned and said, "That summer on the farm, Gene put me in the driver's seat on the tractor, put it in gear, and off I went on my crash course to learn to drive it. I've been waiting to teach you to drive a boat the same way!"

On Friday I found myself in big city traffic as I guided my motor home along an overcrowded I-35 to Waco, Texas, to meet my brother-in-law, Lee Keeney. He was camping there for a weekend of square dancing. Lee and my sister started Camping Squares locally, statewide, and nationally, many years before because they loved to square dance and camp. Even after my sister died, he continued with the group and he even became a square dance and round dance caller. I was only five when they got married, so Lee had always been in my life. My mother and dad died when I was only twenty-four, so Bobbie and Lee played an important part in my life. After a hilarious experience trying to learn how to square dance and eating way too much food, I drove back up to Grapevine Sunday afternoon.

On February 14th, I battened down the hatches in the motor home and headed south on a terribly busy I-35. My brother-in-law, Lee, still lived in Killeen, Texas, as did his youngest daughter, Kathy, and her husband, Tim McPherson, whose driveway soon became my new home. Lee and I didn't have trouble finding things to do during the day while Tim and Kathy worked. Some of the time we would just sit and visit about old times and how hard it was to adjust to living without our spouses.

Tim and Kathy worked for the government, so we made big plans for the three-day President Day weekend. Using my RV, we headed for Kathy's favorite place, the beach. I found out exactly how long Texas was as we spent almost six hours getting to Port Aransas. I discovered a different kind of road as I drove onto a ferry that was part of Highway 361, which took us to Mustang Island. We camped close to the water and became real beach bums. Kathy not only loves beaches but the rule for the weekend was we would eat fish and fresh seafood every meal. I have always enjoyed fishing, so Tim showed me how to do it Texas style, and the results were enough fish for a meal.

While walking along the pier, we talked to a family who had just brought in some fresh oysters. Kathy saw it as my opportunity to taste a raw one for the first time, and since I don't mind trying new food, I was game. They said it was good that these were very fresh and cracked one open for me. The slimy thing slipped down my throat, and the expression on my face was all they needed to see to know that I hadn't enjoyed the experience one bit.

"Oh, you need to try one with a cracker!"

Slurp. Ewwww!

"Try one with this kind of sauce!"

Slurp. Yuck!

"Now try it this way!"

All told, I think I ate four or five of the squidgy things. *Bleahhh!*

We had lots of fun and all-in-all, it was a great weekend experiencing the coastal areas of Texas.

I spent the rest of February in Killen, sharing my time among the family and riding my nice new bike around for exercise.

The first of March, I drove to the hill country of Texas to spend time with my nephew, Bill Keeney, and his wife, Roz. They had built their dream home overlooking Balcones Canyon between Liberty Hill and Marble Falls, where they had privacy but could also enjoy the beauty of the area. I had never been able to get to know them, so I was happy to have time together. They have the same love for the Lord that I do, so most of the days were sharing what God had been doing in our lives. I went with them to church, their small group, Roz's quilting group, and their other activities. On several occasions, we drove around, and they showed me the beauty of their area of Texas. We had such an enjoyable time together that I promised them that I would try and get back to see them before I left the state.

My next stop was only a short distance away because I was on my way to spend more time with Linda's children, Kim, and Mike. Even driving for short distances can be challenging. I found myself in bumper-to-bumper traffic again, trying to keep enough space between me and the car in front to be able to stop quickly. Someone decided to dart in front of me and then slammed on his brakes! Even with my bad knee, I slammed on my brakes so hard that everything else that wasn't nailed down, including my mattress, shifted violently toward the cab. When my rig finally came to a stop, you would not have been able to get a straw between us. I could almost visualize my then very thin angel between the two vehicles taking a deep breath of relief.

That was just one of many times that the Lord protected me.

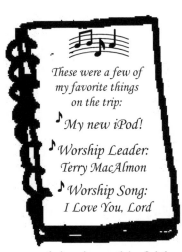

The next month in Texas went fast with a weekend in San Antonio, a photo workshop in the Hill Country, and Easter with family in Killeen. I made one last trip up to Grapevine. (Remember how I felt like the yo-yo going up and down the state?) Over lunch with Bob and Barb, I expressed my desire to listen to my growing collection of CDs while driving. Bob said, "I think I have the perfect solution." He went on to explain about this fairly new device called an "iPod." He shared how easy it was to use, because you download the CDs on the computer and the songs are then transferred to the iPod. It didn't take much to convince me, so we immediately went to buy it and an adapter to use in my cassette player. Because of my love of music, I consider that one of the greatest inventions ever made. I still use it every day.

I sadly pulled out of the driveway on my last day in Texas, April 4th, and got on the road again. My sad mood didn't last long as I began savoring the beautiful praise music vibrating around me and delighting in the gorgeous wildflowers bordering the sides of the road. With the spring rains, the bluebonnets, Indian blankets, black-eyed Susans, and so many more vibrant colored flowers were in glorious bloom. It couldn't get much better than this; God, music, and flowers.

As I was pressing into this wonderful moment, I started to reflect on the many highlights of my Texas trip. The *depth* of this state was not only its beauty but being able to spend special time with family. So many blessings, like gliding along Grapevine Lake in Bob and Barb's sailboat, square dancing with Lee's friends in Waco, or just a quiet evening with Linda, Tim, and Nathan. I loved walking on the beach with Tim and Kathy and the fun of eating the Cajun boiled dinner of jumbo shrimp, crab legs, sausage, potatoes, and small corn that covered my small table. One evening, my great nephew, Mike, took me along on one of his gigs to play percussion for a dance band. I loved the days spent with Bill and Roz and the day trip to the quaint small town of Fredericksburg. What great fun it was to help Kim, my great niece, decorate a castle birthday cake for her husband Bruce. Why a castle birthday cake? Well, her daughter Kendall's birthday was coming up and Bruce got the practice cake. The highlight was when all Lee's children and their families gathered at his home for Easter dinner. Helping the young children look for Easter eggs and fellowshipping around the table with the whole family together is something we will reminisce about for years.

I certainly was enjoying the last of my Texas travels when I slowly pulled out of a curve and viewed a beautiful field of bluebonnets. Seeing a small turn-out area, I slowed my vehicle to a stop so I could get a better look. I sat there a few moments trying to imprint this majestic picture that God had created into my mind. A shaft of sunlight streamed through the clouds, turning the meadow into a shimmering sea of blue. Trees framed the back of the field, but one large oak stood majestically along one side. Not far away was a small bird perched on a weathered tree stump singing a sweet serenade. My eye caught the graceful red paintbrush flowers that were sprinkled through the blanket of blue that sat upon a carpet of green. To top it all off, there were charming butterflies happily flitting around.

I wish I had not been in such a hurry to get to my evening destination. I should have taken the extra time to disembark and enjoy the fragrance of the morning dew still lingering on the flowers, hear the little birds singing, and study the intricate details of the bluebonnets. Since that moment, I have visualized how Jesus and I would have just stood there in reverent awe taking in the elegant splendor of color, savoring the sounds, and feeling the gentle breeze, being quiet and still, and welcoming the glowing feeling of being in each other's presence. What an occasion that would be! Do you know that God wants to spend those special moments with you? This is what it is like to go to new *heights* with God. My desire is to spend this kind of time with God and embrace all He has for me.

Oh, how I wished that I had taken a few more minutes to experience that special moment with God. The times I have gone higher with God have happened when I take the opportunity to sit still, bask in His presence, and soak in His love. I am that busy person who has a list of things that I want to accomplish each day, week, month, and year, but even I have discovered the value of quiet time with God.

The *width* of God's love is so awesome that it reaches around the world. The Bible tells us that in the most familiar Bible verse of John 3:16

> *For God so (greatly) loved and dearly prized the world, that He (even) gave His (one and) only begotten Son, so that whoever believes and trusts in Him (as Savior) shall not perish but have eternal life.*
>
> *John 3:16 (Amplified Bible)*

God's love covers the entire universe. This means He loves each person in every little corner of the world. As I drove, I would look at the faraway horizon and see a mountain range, then look in my rear-view mirror and see nothing but a vast expanse of desolate terrain behind me. No matter how limitless they looked, it would be like a raindrop in the ocean compared to the infinite love of God.

You are a part of that world and I want you to wrap your mind around the reality that God loves you so very much. He has not abandoned you and nothing you have ever done, no matter how bad it is, can diminish the love He has for you. He loves you so very much that He sent His only son into the world to be a sacrifice for your sins. I certainly wasn't a saint and there is a whole list of things I have regretted doing, but because of the width of God's love, I gave those sins to God and He cleansed me through the blood Jesus shed on the cross. If He did this for me, He can do it for you. You are like a precious stone to Him. God is extending His love to you right now. so reach out and accept it. Let God's gold-tinged love wash over you and soak into the depths of your being.

Everywhere I went, I experienced so much love, and the *depth* of that love was overwhelming. All through my life, I have experienced the dimensions of God's love, although I admit there were times when it didn't feel like God was anywhere around. But we can't go on feelings. We must trust and believe His word.

"...and the Lord, He is the One who goes before you. He will be with you. He will not leave you nor forsake you, do not fear nor be dismayed."

Deuteronomy 31:8

This is a promise that we can stand on. He is always with us. Remember the yo-yo? That string was always attached to it. When I was going through various trials, I could really relate to the yo-yo dangling at the end of the string. God seemed a long way from me, but He never let go. As I have read through the many journals I have kept over the last twenty-seven years, there have been many yo-yo experiences. Either my family or I would be going through tribulation and I would plead with God to please help, not really realizing how close He was. It was the times that I would stop focusing so much on the problem and focus more on God and His love that I could feel myself rush firmly back into His hands.

"But seek first the Kingdom of God and His righteousness and all these things shall be added to you."

Matthew 6:33

Seeking Him and immersing ourselves in His love is the most important thing we can do. I had to go through the continual process of learning to trust Him by putting situation after situation in His hands. I had to learn to relax, to stop worrying, to let go of trying to control the situation, and start praising Him for what He was doing. The more I focused on God's endless love and basked in His presence, the easier it was to go through the trial because I wasn't doing it on my own anymore.

I love this verse:

> *"But LORD, your endless love stretches from one eternity to the other, unbroken and unrelenting toward those who fear You and those who bow face down in awe before You. Your faithfulness to keep every gracious promise you've made passes from parents, to children, to grandchildren, and beyond."*
>
> *Psalm 103:17 (TPT)*

Isn't it awesome that His endless love stretches from one eternity to the other, or from everlasting to everlasting? That's pretty long!!! I am also very thankful for His faithfulness to keep His promises not only to us but to our children, grandchildren and beyond. What a wonderful promise not only for us, but for all the generations that follow. This is a promise I want you to hold on to.

The depth I found in Texas was not only in the ethnic diversity of its people but was the wonderful opportunity to spend quality time with my nieces and nephews and their families. We were always a close family, but when my sister passed away suddenly in 1998, it was all the more critical to spend time together. I was very thankful that I finally had the opportunity to get better acquainted with them. The time I was able to be in their homes, learn what they enjoyed doing, talk about their work, or just experience the fun activities they enjoyed doing was all incredibly special to me.

This is the same as our relationship with God. The more time we spend with Him, the better we know and understand Him as God the Father, Jesus the Son, and our constant companion, the Holy Spirit. I wanted and still want to know God in a deeper way and to be saturated with the fullness of God, Jesus, and Holy Spirit. There had been occasions in my life when I was able to get away for one or two days to have some one-on-one time with God at various mini-retreats, which have always been wonderful.

While I was visiting Roz, we talked about a spiritual experience she had been touched by called Silent Retreats. As you might imagine, they are a special time for women to take a break from busy lives and encounter God. Long story short, I ended up facilitating them for three years in Arizona and then one in Idaho for my friends there.

My friend Larry said that a woman's silent retreat was an oxymoron.

You would be surprised what women can do when they have an intense hunger for God.

In 2015, I invited Pastor Danny Mullins to be our spiritual director. He taught us different kinds of prayers and was able to take things to an even deeper level. It is like when you are enjoying a moist carrot cake and are very satisfied until someone adds the cream cheese frosting and then you realize how much better it is.

Pastor Mullins taught us the importance of centering, or contemplative, prayer. Centering prayer is simply a way of praying designed to keep us centered on God's presence. In Bill Volkman's book, *Basking in His Presence,* he explains it like this: "We come to God in love to be fully attentive to His presence within." (Volkman, 101.) We focus our mind on nothing but His presence.

"Be still and know that I am God."

Psalm 46:10

Here are some practical instructions on the process of centering prayer:

1. Choose a sacred word or phrase to use as a point of focus. Examples: Abba, Father, Jesus, Holy Spirit, love, peace, rest, etc. I am currently using love.

2. Sit comfortably in a quiet place, close your eyes, and open your heart to God and the Holy Spirit, and introduce the sacred word. Your sacred word will become so natural that it will be more of a sigh than a pronounced word.
3. Each time you realize your mind has drifted, call your attention back to the word or phrase.
4. Every time you call your attention back to Him, it is an act of worship.

Volkman adds, "Instead of, or in addition to, a sacred word, you may be led to use a sacred glance. You may find that a simple image will best bring you back to an awareness of God's presence." (Volkman, 48.) An example would be Mary sitting at the feet of Jesus, or you as a child running into the arms of Jesus. I visualize Jesus walking with me in an amazing flower garden. God has given us an imagination and it's our job to try to keep our minds and spirits as pure as possible, but with the Holy Spirit's help to use our imagination properly. It's our sanctified imagination. I visualize that Jesus is with me and there is nothing wrong with that because He *is* with me and He loves the time I spend with Him.

> *"I pray that the light of God will illuminate the eyes of your imagination, flooding you with light, until you experience the full revelation of the hope of His calling---that is, the wealth of God's glorious inheritances that He finds in us, His holy ones."*
>
> *Ephesians 1:18 (TPT)*

"When we practice God's presence in centering prayer, our intention is precisely this: to do nothing. Our only desire is to be with our Lover, to 'hang out' with Him." (Volkman, 100.)

We need to recognize God as the initiator—and our only purpose is to give our total attention to His presence in us. Later on, we can ask Him questions, but the starting place is to spend time with Jesus and allow Him to speak to us. As of this moment I have not heard the audible voice of God or seen an open vision, but I do hear God and I do visualize Jesus with me. Then, I ask Jesus questions and listen for that still small voice to see what His answer is.

> *"There's a private place reserved for the lovers of God, where they sit near him and receive the revelation-secrets of His promises."*
>
> *Psalm 25:14 (TPT)*

I will give you an example of one of my centering times. I usually set a timer, so I don't have to worry about the time. You could start with five or ten minutes, but soon you'll want to go longer. After the centering time, I like to write about what happened in my journal. This is from my journal on January 1, 2016. I was home alone and excited that I was going to spend all morning with God, and I had no time limitations. I usually start with praise and worship then meditate on His Word.

> *Why does it seem that I have to be in control of things?*
>
> *After spending some quiet time with Jesus, I saw myself on the seat of a covered wagon and I was frantically trying to control the four horses with the mess of reins in my hands. They were prancing around, and I wasn't having any success in controlling them. Jesus was sitting on the seat next to me and He held out His hands as if to indicate, "Do you want me to try?" When I gave Him the reins, the horses immediately calmed down. He had just been sitting there waiting for me to give Him the reins and the control. He wanted me to sit back, relax, and enjoy the scenery—the creek meandering through the field of wildflowers, and the snowcapped mountains in the distance. He said, "I don't want you burdened down with tasks. I've always wanted you to run with freedom and enjoy the world I have made."*

Since that day, I have been better about trying not to control things. If I do see myself trying to take control of a situation, I just think back to that picture and then turn the reins back over to God.

Another source that I found helpful was *Finding Father: A Journey into the Loving Arms of Daddy God*, by A.J. Jones. It is a twelve-week study.

In it, A.J. Jones says, "Soaking and resting in His presence has made the biggest difference in my personal walk with God. God is hungry for your time, He desires your company, and He wants to speak to you. He is not interested in merely telling you 'stuff', but rather in sharing His Heart and hearing yours."

Heidi Baker, who runs a huge ministry of outreach to the people of Mozambique, says, "All fruitfulness flows out of intimacy with God."

I am very engaged with my church and keep busy with various activities. I am on an intercessory prayer team for a large ministry. I participate in seminars and retreats. I have my daily devotional readings and am in a mentoring group.

I am convinced that the few minutes I spend each day in centering prayer has been more life-changing than all my other spiritual practices.

In my journey of life, I have made many wonderful friends and have developed lasting relationships, but the most intimate relationship I want nourish is the one I have with my God. My desire for each of you is that you will:

> *"...experience the great magnitude of the astonishing love of Christ in all its dimensions. How deeply intimate and far-reaching is His love! How enduring and inclusive it is!"*
>
> *Ephesians 3:16 (TPT)*

I want you to know without a doubt, deep down in your heart, that God is so extremely in love with you and He is waiting to spend some special time with you.

The Keeney Family, Easter 2005.

For
I am the Lord
who heals you.

Exodus 15:26

Chapter Twelve

Highway to Healing

After the beautiful drive through the hill country, it still took a day and a half of driving through west Texas before I finally exited that awesome state. While staying in an RV Park in Fort Stockton, a fellow RV-er gave me a high recommendation for a great RV park in Las Cruces, New Mexico, so that was my destination that evening. As I entered the city, I took the exit they had given me.

> *Oh, look! A Walmart! I think I'll stop and pick up a few groceries.*

The Walmart was located on Valley Road, the same road the campground was on. I slowly maneuvered my rig out of the driveway to turn right. I had noticed a policeman parked in the Walmart lot and considered asking him for directions, but I was a mail lady for years! If anyone could find an address, it would be me.

Hmmmm.... the sun is going down. I sure hope I can find this place quickly. It's so hard to set up camp after it gets dark.

Hmmmm...the address numbers on the buildings aren't anywhere close to the numbers I'm looking for.

Hmmmm...somehow, I'm back at I-10. I guess I'll try again.

I maneuvered my 27' motor home through the busy evening traffic of Las Cruces, making small circles, large circles, square circles, and so many circles, I lost count. At one point I stopped to look up the number of the campground in the phone book, but, to my dismay when I called, their answering machine clicked on. Feeling utterly lost, I pulled myself up behind the wheel and with tears in my eyes, asked the Lord what I should do.

I drove back to Valley Road, but this time I was traveling in the opposite direction.

Hey! That sign said NORTH Valley Road—I must have been on South Valley Road before. The address I want is on North Valley Road! Aaargh—if I'd only turned LEFT out of the Walmart lot, I would have already been there with my camp all set up by now. Ugh.

Why hadn't I taken a moment and asked the policeman or even stopped at a gas station and asked for directions, instead of trying to do it all on my own? Why didn't I ask for God's help sooner?

I'm thinking about how easy this all would have been if I had my modern-day smartphone with GPS. I did finally pull into the park, very tired and disappointed with myself for the choices I had made. This certainly wasn't the first time on the trip that I had made poor choices. Why hadn't I learned from my previous experiences?

The next morning, I was sitting outside having my morning coffee and observing what a charming park it was. It didn't take me long to decide it was the perfect time to take a day off from driving and just rest. My whole trip had been going from one place to the next, one group of people to the next, and not taking much "me time." The motor home needed to be serviced and a vent cover had to be replaced, so this would be the perfect opportunity to get that done. Hadn't I just learned a lesson about taking time, especially quiet time with God?

That afternoon I was sitting under a beautiful shade tree, reflecting on what had happened the night before and how that related to most of my life. How many times in my life had I been going around in circles, doing the same thing over and over hoping and praying that the next time would produce different results?

My Spiritual Journey

I loved the merry-go-round when I was a child and my life reminded me of those times, only there always came a time in childhood when I was dizzy and tired and wanted to get off. The merry-go-round of my life had gone in the same circle for years. Every January 1st, I would write the same goals:

1. Clean out the paper clutter in my office.
2. Lose weight.
3. Exercise more.
4. Wish and pray for a better marriage and that my husband would accept Christ into his life.
5. Pray and hope that my children and grandchildren would choose to walk the path God has for them.

I am sure some of you can relate to these continual goals and prayer needs, but there were some deeper emotional scars that caused me to go around in circles year after year.

During my mail-carrying days, I had my designated forty-four-mile route that I traveled every day. I went in the same direction, completing the same circle five or six days a week for the nineteen years that I was employed in that job. There was a good reason for this because that was the most efficient and orderly way of completing the job. I am sure that some of you have jobs where it is necessary to do something that is repetitive, but in life, do you want to keep making wrong decisions over and over?

I have known people who have spouses or maybe children who are addicted to drugs and alcohol. They pray that they will come out of that lifestyle and finally go to a treatment center and get clean. They are overjoyed when it happens and take them back into their lives, only to be crushed again, months later, when they start using again. Sometimes this happens again and again, and they wonder what they can do to stop this tragic circle. I learned a long time ago that I have no control over the decisions that my children or husband might make, but there are things I can do to help myself. I can choose a better way to respond to their choices.

I eventually found out that I had emotional wounds that needed to be healed. I think everyone has some type of emotional wounding. It might be unforgiveness, trauma, trust, abandonment, physical or mental abuse, rejection, shame, or it might be something unknown that has come down through the generations.

Part of my problems came from holding on to wounds.

"So we must let go of every wound that has pierced us (every arrow tip in us) and the sin we so easily fall into."

Hebrews 12:1 (TPT)

We need to let go of every wound, so my first thought is, "Yes, I want every wound out of my life, doesn't everyone?" Why would we want to hold on to it? Why would we want to continue to carry a painful arrow tip around with us? But, when I thought back over most of my life, I realized that that is exactly what I did. I never forgot any hurtful word spoken in anger by my husband, or a belittling remark said to me or the children. I didn't let go of those hurts and wounds. I would continue to play that hurt over and over in my mind. I would tell close friends so they could pray for me, which is a good thing, but I realized that it was not only prayer but sympathy that I wanted. I was feeling sorry for myself and I wanted others to feel sorry for me, too. I also found out later that relating a hurtful story was, in fact, dishonoring my husband. This went on for too many years. Was I happy in this continuous cycle? No!!! Why did I continue to do the same things over and over? I needed help to know how to get rid of the wounds. By the time I did learn about how I could be set free, the arrows were embedded so deep that I didn't know if I wanted to go through the pain of pulling them out.

The first thing, after recognizing the problem was that I had to decide that I wanted to get rid of the arrow in my heart, that deep, emotional wound. If anyone literally had an arrow tip or bullet in their body, they would go to a doctor to have it removed. When we have a deep soul wound that needs to be healed why not go to someone that can help us get rid of that wound so we can have true freedom? All the issues of life flow from our soul (mind, will, and emotions.) This is the part of your life that Satan will target. This is where the battle takes place. I try and make a daily choice not to let him control my thoughts, feelings, and decisions. Instead, I keep my eyes on God and declare His Word. The more of the glory light of Jesus that is in me,

155

the less room there is for Satan and his lies. Be sure to ask God for wisdom when it is time to search out trained individuals. They will help you find freedom from past hurts and get rid of the lies the enemy has been feeding you.

God wants us to live in freedom.

"For with God, nothing will be impossible."

Luke 1:37

Recently, I have been able to experience the incredible freedom of having my soul and spiritual wounds healed. God wants us to have real and lasting healing. During the years when I was going through trying times, it would have been so helpful to have someone with more knowledge than I had to walk through the emotional healing with me. I did go to some counselors and took self-help classes that were helpful, but I needed more. I am thankful that I now have training in healing deep emotional wounds so I can help others experience freedom. How I wished I had known about this years ago!

The first training I had was Immanuel Prayer. This is one of the prayers that Danny Mullins taught us at the silent retreat. The Immanuel prayer approach helps us connect to God in very tangible ways and removes the barriers that keep us from enjoying intimacy with Christ.

A few years ago, Ruth Hendrickson came to Arizona for an in-depth emotional healing and deliverance ministry training called Mashah. It was developed by Ruth to bring people into new levels of personal freedom through healing past hurts and wounds. It also brings you into a new realm of intimacy with God—a realm of healing and empowerment.

Just recently, I was trained to be an issue-focused minister with Restoring the Foundations or RTF. The ministry was developed twenty years ago by Chester and Betsy Kylstra. RTF is a Spirit-led adventure which provides people with an opportunity to receive God's freedom and healing from guilt, shame, anger, and pain. It's a very in-

156

depth healing program, and part of it is the same process I had learned in Immanuel Prayer. It also brings to light any ungodly lies a person might be listening to and teaches people to replace them with the truth of God's word. It is a program where you can experience true deliverance.

I learned important information with all three of these programs and they gave me much-needed freedom from emotional wounds. God is the one who does the healing, just as it is with physical healings that come from prayer. I learned to have intimacy with the Lord and listen to the Holy Spirit for what needs to be healed. Then He does it. I tried to practice walking in the continual presence of the Lord so I could abide with an interactive connection with Jesus as I walk through life.

I am sure there are many good courses out there, but these are the ones I am familiar with. Whatever method or ministry you decide to use, be sure the Holy Spirit is the instructor and teacher.

> *"I will instruct you and teach you in the way which you should go; I will counsel you with My eye upon you."*
>
> *Psalm 32:8 (NASB)*

God does not want us to continually go in circles over deeply rutted paths. He can and will lead us on fresh trails of adventure. What we need to do is stay in communication with God and follow His guiding presence.

Physical wounds are much easier to heal, generally speaking, than the hurts to our hearts. It's these emotional wounds that people lug around for a lifetime. Don't continue to carry them around. There is help out there for you to receive total freedom from any past hurts and soul wounds. If you are carrying around scars from life, my prayer for you is to get some help as soon as possible, so you can live in freedom and become the person God wants you to be.

*"We are products of our past, but we don't have
to be prisoners of it."*

Rick Warren

L-R: Julie, David, Donna, Karma, Gene

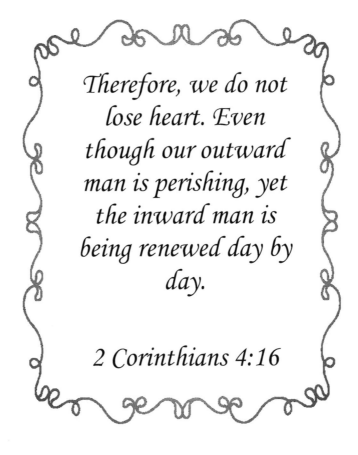

Therefore, we do not lose heart. Even though our outward man is perishing, yet the inward man is being renewed day by day.

2 Corinthians 4:16

Chapter Thirteen

Adventures Awaiting Seniors

The day's rest had been wonderful, and I felt refreshed and rejuvenated to experience all that Arizona might have for me.

The drive through eastern Arizona was not all that exciting.

That section of I-10 is fairly flat with a sprinkling of cactus dotting the dry, desert landscape. I still enjoyed the bright blue sky as I sang along with the praise and worship music vibrating through the cab. I started to think back about all the various places I had been in the last six and a half months. So far, there hadn't been any certain place or ministry that God had highlighted to me. Before I had started on the trip, I had read Rick Warren's book, *The Purpose Driven Life*. I learned that God had made me into a special "SHAPE": Spiritual gifts, Heart, Ability, Personality, and Experience. (Warren, 2002.) I envisioned myself as this multifaceted object rolling around the

United States, trying to find the perfectly-made chamber that God had prepared for me. I knew that God had an ideal place, but most importantly, God had put a certain calling on my life and I wanted to find what that was. I continually prayed for God's direction.

I spent my first night in Arizona right outside of Tucson visiting the Bylers, who had been my neighbors in Idaho. It was good to catch up with what had been happening in each of our lives.

The next morning after a leisurely breakfast, I headed up to Mesa. Mary Lee Smith, a mail carrier friend from Idaho, lived in Mesa and had invited me to come spend a couple of weeks at her 55+ plus community. This was the first time I was able to experience the leisurely lifestyle of many retired seniors. I thoroughly enjoyed all the many activities: playing cards, water aerobics, and neighborhood get-togethers. Communities like this have such a variety of fun things to do. This lifestyle option could be very appealing, but my earnest desire was to be in some kind of ministry and be obedient to what God wanted me to do. I had considered living close to my children, especially my grandchildren in Michigan, but I concluded that I should have many good years left to serve God. I wanted a new adventure with Him, and I wanted to be sure I was going to be accomplishing the work He called me to do.

In August of 2004, while getting ready for the trip, I received a call from Harry Bolwyn, a pastor who was starting a new church in Casa Grande, Arizona. He asked if I would come and help him and his wife, Margie, with the church plant they were doing. I explained that I had planned this extended trip, but I would stop and visit with them when I got to Arizona. When I called to arrange the best time, he wanted me to be there on a Sunday so I could visit the church. He also recommended I stay at Palm Creek Golf and RV Park, so it was late Saturday afternoon when I pulled into that gorgeous campground. I slowly maneuvered my motor home between large palm trees.

Wow! I have never stayed in any park this beautiful!

Harry and Margie came over Saturday evening for a short visit and said they had arranged for someone to pick me up the next morning for church. It was a Christian Missionary Alliance church and that was the denomination I had been going to in Twin Falls. I found the people were wonderful. Some of us went to lunch after church so we could get better acquainted. Lois Carrick, who was staying at Palm Creek, had joined us, so after lunch, she offered to take me to see some interesting places in the area. We had a whole afternoon of fun!

As I lay in bed that night reflecting on all that happened that day, I was wondering if I had finally found the niche that God had designed for me. I liked the Oasis church, the pastor, his wife, and the people I had met. I even made a new friend. The town and area seemed inviting and the RV park was better than I ever dreamed possible. I peacefully drifted off to sleep after that awesome day.

The next weekend, I left my motor home at Mary Lee's park and flew to San Antonio, Texas. for a wedding reception. This gave me the opportunity to see all the Keeney clan one more time. I shared with them pictures of Palm Creek and the ministry opportunity that had opened up for me. My nephew Bill jokingly asked, "And Hawaii was not available?" I asked them to pray with me about the decision I needed to make.

My two weeks in Arizona had been very eventful. I was able to experience what the retirement lifestyle was like. I saw friends and spent an evening with my niece, Bea Day. Mary Lee had taken me to Sedona for a day, and there was a ministry opportunity that had opened up to me. Was this going to be the special place God had for me? While in Arizona, I had no accidents or motor home breakdowns and that was a real plus.

I left Arizona feeling blessed.

My Spiritual Journey

I was never worried about getting older because my mind was still sharp, I was in good health, and I had a positive, courageous outlook on life. I saw the world as full of wonderful potential opportunities, and I knew for sure that I didn't want to sit in a rocking chair and watch the world pass me by. I wanted to try a new and different venture.

Discovering what other seniors have accomplished has been encouraging for me.

In the Bible, there are several examples of people starting new careers after they are seventy years old. Abraham was seventy-five years old when he and his whole household left Haran to go to Canaan land. Talk about relocating! That was on foot with maybe a donkey or a camel to ride, and I'm sure he didn't have much of a map to follow. Think how much easier it would have been for him if he'd had a GPS! And what about his wife, Sarah, traipsing around in the wilderness with only a tent to sleep in at sixty-five.

Moses was eighty when he led the Israelites out of Egypt, which was no picnic. He spent the next forty years having the responsibility of managing a large group of complaining, fearful people. What was so wonderful was the special encounters he had with God and all this happened after he was eighty years old.

Caleb was eighty-five when he went back into the Promised Land, forty-five years after his first visit. He said, "I am still as strong today as I was in the day Moses sent me; as my strength was then, so my strength is now…" (Joshua 14:11.) This tells me that they did some pretty awesome things in their later years.

Each one of these individuals had a calling on their lives and God guided them through their own special journey.

I have learned that I need to live with an eternal perspective. One day I will appear before the judgment seat of Christ and I want to be sure I have accomplished all He has called me to do.

"For we must all appear before the judgment seat of Christ so that each one may be recompensed for his deeds in the body, according to what he has done, whether good or bad."

2 Corinthians 5:10 (NASB)

This verse really hit home in my heart. I wanted to be sure I was not only doing His will, but I also needed to watch my thoughts, words, motives, and intentions. The examples from the Bible were all seventy or older, but this verse applies to EVERYONE, no matter what their age.

The questions I was asking were:

God, what is my calling?

What ministry do you have for me?

What is that dream opportunity I finally have time to pursue?

"Where there is no vision, the people perish."

Proverbs 29:18 (KJV)

God created us to dream, imagine, and envision, so our dreams are important and it's God's desire to help us achieve them. It's never too late to fulfill a dream that you have put on the back burner. The famous artist Grandma Moses (Anna Mary Robertson Moses) did not even pick up a paint brush until she was seventy-six years old and was still painting at 100. ("Grandma Moses", n.d.)

Sister Madonna Buder, known as the Iron Nun, holds the title of the oldest women ever to finish an Ironman Triathlon, which she ran at age 82. Sister Buder is still competing and winning triathlons at the age of 88. It is people like this who encourage me not to give up and to believe that I am not too old to start living a new dream.

I really like this quote:

"The only place your dream becomes impossible is
in your own thinking."

Robert Schuller (Brainy Quote)

I like the story of Dorothy Steel, who went to acting school in her mid-eighties and became a professional actress at eighty-eight. At ninety-one. she landed the role of the Merchant Tribal Elder in the Black Panther movie, which became one of the best-selling movies in the world. In a Washington Post article, Steel said, "Keep your mind open and keep faith in yourself that you can do this thing. All you have to do is step out there and try it. And if you don't make it on the first step, step out there again and you'll find something you can step out on, but don't just sit back. Life is not just about sitting back. Life is about stepping out'. (*She started acting at 88. Four years later, she's recognized everywhere for Black Panther*. The Washington Post, March 23, 2018, by Kelyn Soong 2018)

This is what my whole trip was about. I was stepping out and trying something new and different. I had certainly stepped out of the comfort zone of my small-town life to travel alone, not knowing what might be ahead. It hadn't been easy, and I could have given up several times, but I kept going.

"At times, we don't know what to do, but quitting is not an option."

2 Corinthians 4:8b

I just knew in my heart that God had something special for me to do and a unique calling for my life. God had been preparing me for sixty-two years for such a time as this. He taught me to be a leader through the many organizations I served in. I learned to be a servant by helping the less fortunate and welcoming people into my home. In my postal carrier job, I was trained to be a facilitator for the Quality of Worklife program and served as an area facilitator for three years. I was able to improve my teaching skills when I taught the new rural carriers and special training classes to postal employees. God had been continually pruning away negative habits and replacing them with His wisdom, so I would become the person He had designed me to be. God's desire was for me to produce quality fruit for His kingdom.

I thought back to my years growing up on an apple orchard. My dad had planted the trees many years before, but they were still producing much fruit, even as they were getting old. He watered them regularly and pruned them every spring and because of his tender love and care, they continued to produce large high-quality apples. John 15:1-8 tells us that Jesus is the true vine and His Father is the vine-grower, or farmer. We need to be pruned to be productive branches and "as we live in union with Jesus as our source, fruitfulness will stream from within." (John 15:5b, TPT.)

I was looking forward to many years of a fruitful, productive life.

As a senior, I needed to remind myself that I am not too old to learn. I am thankful that God continually puts new growing opportunities in front of me. Don't ever get to the point where you think you know it all. As it turned out, there was a new avenue of learning that He wanted me to experience that I almost missed out on.

When I was looking for a spiritual director for our 2015 silent retreat, I had several phone conversations with Lauretta Clark. She had explained that she was in her first year of the two-year training to become a spiritual director, so was still learning. One morning, she called and shared a little about what spiritual direction was and wondered if I would be willing to meet with her once a month. She needed a few people to practice on, so the only cost for me would be the gas for the hour drive to her home. I said I would need to pray about it.

At first, I wondered if it would be something that would be that beneficial for me. I had led Bible studies and small groups. I was pretty faithful with my Bible reading and prayer, and I was very busy "serving" God. After several conversations with the Holy Spirit, I knew that this was something that He wanted me to do. Just like on my trip when I needed to be open to where God wanted me to go, now I needed to be open to different ways of experiencing that deeper relationship with Him. It ended up being a wonderful year-and-a-half journey and I am so very thankful that I didn't miss out on the blessings I received. Lauretta was a very good director, teaching me different methods of prayers, and with the Holy Spirit's direction, showed me how I could develop a more intimate relationship with God.

I can now pour into others what she poured into me. Keep yourself open to learning opportunities that come up.

As I was heading for California on a busy I-10, my thoughts kept going back to the possibility of living in Arizona and helping Harry and Margie with the church. I had never done anything like this before. Was it something that I would be qualified to do? There was still so much I needed to learn. Would there be an opportunity to grow spiritually while serving others? Wasn't my trip a great example of growing close to God, while experiencing a new adventure?

I thought back to things I had learned:

When I spent time praising and worshiping God, my attitude was better.

That the "the Lord is my strength and song." (Exodus 15:2)

The importance of having a childlike faith.

The importance of family and friends.

God had been with me through it all.

I came from a family who didn't talk about retiring. My dad was still planning on harvesting another apple crop when he died in the spring of 1967 at seventy-four. Pat, my brother, whom I was on my way to visit in California, was still going strong at seventy-eight. As a CPA, he was still doing taxes for some of his special clients and served as the Missions team coordinator for his church. He also was supporting many missionaries all over the world. He is a great example of being fruitful for God.

Age is just a number. Think young and have fun! If you want a few laughs, look up the "Red Hot Mamas" from Coeur d'Alene, Idaho. They are an energetic, uplifting, inspirational group that motivates women to be all they want to be. They are a fun and entertaining group. God's desire for you is to be all that He created you to be.

I want to be sure that my "inner man is being renewed day by day" (2 Corinthians 4:16b). My goal is to stay young-at-heart, to continually learn about God and my fellow man, to eat healthy, and to look with anticipation for every new adventure my Heavenly Father has for me just around the corner.

Me golfing at Palm Creek Golf and RV Park.

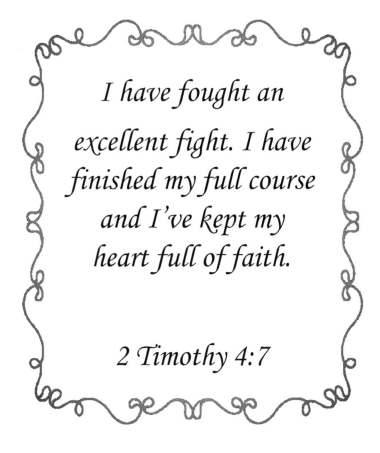

*I have fought an
excellent fight. I have
finished my full course
and I've kept my
heart full of faith.*

2 Timothy 4:7

Chapter Fourteen

The Drive to Finish Well

I had finally made it to California, but now I found myself sitting in a room full of people waiting to see a doctor. A lady across the room was reading a magazine and the couple next to her were visiting. Sitting to my left was my niece, Colette Cozean. I appreciated her support and knowledge because she works in the medical field and was instrumental in getting me an appointment with this outstanding doctor. Colette was busy on her computer, so I started thinking about what had brought me here.

I'd had a fantastic eight months. On my trip, I had seen so many beautiful parts of the country and had fun visiting family and friends. What I hadn't been prepared for were the unforeseen events that tested my courage, fortitude, and abilities. The journey had its mountains, valleys, waterfalls, unexpected curves, detours, and, of course, the continual road construction. There had been the delay in Colorado where my motor home went through a major reconstruction, and since then, it had gone through several repair jobs. Now I was the one who needed a repair job!

The sound of the door opening in the waiting room interrupted my thoughts. The nurse stepped out and called another name. Colette was still concentrating on her work.

As I drifted back into my thoughts, I remembered how I had so looked forward to my California visit. My oldest brother, Pat, had lived here for over fifty years, and now I had time to do some interesting activities with him and his wife, Elsa. My motor home was parked in their front driveway, and they even had an extra car for me. Everything would have been great if I hadn't had that occasional pain in my right knee. I tried to remember when it really started. There was that time when I tried to stand, and my right knee would not bend without pain. It started out as an occasional incident, but with the continued use of my right leg, it was happening more often. I remembered the episode where the car pulled in front of me in Austin, Texas, and I slammed on my brakes. My reaction was fast, despite the excruciating pain. Being a farm wife, I had learned to press on even if I was hurt.

A question from Colette brought me back into the waiting room. As I looked up, the nurse entered and called my name. When Dr. Yocum finally came into the room and showed us the x-rays, we could see that there was a definite tear in the meniscus that was causing the pain. He also pointed out significant cartilage decay. I agreed to have him do arthroscopic surgery to repair and clean around the knee because I didn't want a total knee replacement at that time.

The doctor's office had scheduled the surgery for a few weeks out, so I still had time to do some fun things. The last three weeks had flown by quickly. The company Julie works for, JCB, has their main office in Los Angeles. She was in town for Mother's Day weekend, so we had a great time with family. Pat and Elsa took me to several gardens and other points of interest. I was looking forward to a weekend in Fresno visiting a cousin I hadn't seen for forty-eight years.

I couldn't believe that it was finally time to leave California. Driving on the crazy California freeways made me anxious to get back to my Idaho home with the McNurlins. My knee surgery went well, but I was going to take it slow going home. I planned on spending a couple of nights with friends in Nevada to give my knee a rest.

I knew that my wonderful, exciting, amazing trip would soon be ending. I had seen many beautiful areas of our country and had enjoyed visiting family and friends. I especially relished the alone time I had with God, but it was time to get back home to Idaho.

# of days driving: 43

# of miles driven: 10,677

# of times having a GPS would have come in handy:

SO MANY!

My Spiritual Journey

It was a sunny June day as I was traveling through desolate Nevada and I had plenty of time to reflect on the last nine months. I knew that God had been with me.

> *"Behold I am with you and will keep you wherever you go and will bring you back to this land for I will not leave you until I have done what I have promised you"*
>
> *Genesis 28:15*

I confidently believed this promise of God, and that He was with me through the trip. He was there as I enjoyed the beautiful fall colors in Michigan, the quaint country roads in North Carolina, and the hills covered with bluebonnets in Texas. He was there when I had the accident in Colorado, on the bridge in Michigan when the wind hit the motor home, and in the operating room in California. I sensed His presence as I was traveling on those bright sunny days listening to praise and worship music and enjoying His creation. He was with me on those dark cold nights in Kentucky and Tennessee when I didn't feel His presence, but I clung to His promise that He would never leave me or forsake me.

I thought back to the many times God had been there with me in Idaho. God was there during my husband's first heart attack and the tragedy of having to quit farming. He was there in the decisions about what we were going to do next, and how we would generate an income. He was with me through the many, dark, cloudy emotions of not feeling loved or appreciated. There were the special times when I could feel Gods presence, but there were also the times when I had no feeling at all, and I just had to trust the promise that He was with me.

God was with me through the joyful times of playing with my children, and the mountain vacations where we would explore remote mountain trails and stop to fish by gently flowing streams. I am sure God was delighted to see all the fun we were having, when our family and friends gathered around our large dining room table devouring a delicious home-cooked meal. As I picked fresh bouquets of flowers from the garden to enhance my beautiful home, I could feel His presence with me.

All these experiences have been part of my spiritual road trip. I had to come to the realization that God has always been with me. I have enjoyed the happy, exciting times of absorbing His presence and the quality times of getting to know God on a deeper, more intimate level. I thank Him for the hard times when He was molding me into the person He knew I could be. I grew so much through all my journeys as He was developing character in me.

> *"God's promise to Joseph purged his character until it was time for his dreams to come true."*
>
> *Psalm 105:19 (TPT)*

During the forty-two years of marriage, God built character in me just like He did in Joseph. I look back on all the things in my life, good and bad, and now realize that God used all of this to build my character until it was time to fulfill the dreams He had for me. I thought about the many times He was building my character during my recent road trip. I learned that I could survive the major repairs that needed to be done on the vehicle, as well as the daily chores of emptying the sewer and water tanks and securing things before I started driving for the day. I learned to press on during tricky situations and to take time to build relationships. I developed courage and fortitude that gave me the confidence that I can do anything with

God's help. I realized that God was making me into the person that He knew I could become. That takes time and isn't usually very easy.

I am extremely thankful that He never gave up on me, but faithfully kept giving me His hand to guide me. There were times I wanted to give up on myself, but He never gave up on me. He has filled me with His everlasting love and light so I can share this with others. I want others to experience His love, light, and glory. I thank God for healing my deepest soul wounds so I can experience true freedom. I know that He wants everyone to find this wonderful freedom from past hurts so they can fulfill their dreams and become all that God has for them.

I was excited to see the "Welcome to Idaho" sign. I finally made it back home! What an eventful trip! Now I was almost back where I started after 267 days and 10,677 miles of travel. Through my entire trip, I kept my focus on Jesus. My recent travels reminded me of how important it is to keep my focus on Him. The ability to get through my journey was to keep my focus on the road. I was aware of vehicles coming out of side roads, cars dodging in and out around me, and rain pounding the windshield, but through it all, I had to stay focused on the road. In life, my focus will always be to keep my eyes on God through the good times and the difficult circumstances, no matter what I may go through.

I am very thankful for the glory light of Jesus that will always be traveling with me.

One of my life verses is Colossians 1:28-29 and I love how the Passion translation says it:

> "Christ is our message! We preach to awaken hearts and bring every person into the full understanding of truth. It has become my inspiration and passion in ministry to labor with a tireless intensity, with His power flowing through me, to present every believer the revelation of being his perfect one in Jesus Christ".

He wants you to be His perfect one in Christ. He longs to have a deeper love relationship with you. As you repeat this prayer, let Him into your heart to heal any hurts and guide you on the path He has for you.

> *God, I thank you for Jesus, who came and died for me so I will no longer live in darkness, but in Your light. I am longing to enter into a deeper place of fellowship with You. Lead me into that secret place where my heart and spirit will be entwined with Your love, light, and glory. Take all the broken bits and pieces of my life and turn them into a beautiful masterpiece of love and devotion to You. I ask that Your light will infuse my dreams with life and gradually transform them into the calling you have for me. It is my heart's desire to live my life so close to You that I will not miss the path You have for me".*

All the paths God has had me on and all the ones that are yet to come are my highway to heaven. He impressed on me that no matter how rough, steep, rocky, or desolate the road might be in my life journey, that it does not even begin to compare to the joys awaiting me in heaven. The Bible gives me a glimpse of the glorious, marvelous splendor of love and light that fills every corner of my final home.

> *"For I consider that the sufferings of this present time are not worthy to be compared with the glory that is to be revealed to us".*
>
> *Romans 8:18 (NASB)*

I hope that through experiencing this journey with me that you have come into a deeper relationship with God and you will now be experiencing the glory light of Jesus in a more intimate way. Remember that God will ALWAYS be with you, keep your eyes focused on Him, and look forward with anticipation to the new journey He has for you.

"He called me out of darkness to experience His marvelous light and now He claims me as His very own. He did this so that I would broadcast His glorious wonders throughout the world."

Adapted from Peter 2:9b (TPT)

Donna, Elsa, and Pat, Laguna Beach, CA 2005.

EPILOGUE

When I found Gene's body in our family room that day, one of my first thoughts was that I wasn't sure that he had gone to heaven.

When we were married, Gene and I were on the same path with our knowledge of God. We had both been raised in the Methodist church and when we were dating, he always went to church with me. After we were married, he found more excuses not to go.

I have to work.

I'm too tired.

I just don't feel like going today.

In 1969, when I asked Jesus into my life, he wasn't happy with all the new Christian activities I wanted to do. He would allow me to go, but when I would come home from an activity, like a Lay Witness Mission weekend, I would never know what his attitude would be when I got there. No matter what I said or shared with him, he wasn't buying what God or I had to offer. I asked him about the obvious change in my brother's life when he had given his life to the Lord and Gene's comment was, "He just wanted to change."

My continual prayer was for Gene to give his life to God. It had been ten years since I had made my commitment and I wanted him to experience the same joy I had. One afternoon, I curled up on the couch with my new book, *You Can Be the Wife of a Happy*

Husband, by Darien B Cooper. I loved the title and I was hoping that this would be the answer to my prayers. As I was reading the Biblical principles she gave to transform a marriage, it wasn't at all what I thought it would be. I was thinking that my *husband* was the one that needed to change, but Darien proceeded to explain how *I* was the one that needed to do things differently. I needed to stop pushing so much and pray more and let God move in his heart. At an Aglow retreat, I had received a prophecy that I was to be like a beautiful rose in a vase on the table. I was to be seen and admired by my husband, but not to preach or nag. By this time, he was only going to church for special occasions.

One beautiful spring evening in 1997, with the trees in blossom and flowers popping out, I was so excited and thankful to be riding with Gene in his pick-up to Rick and Elva McNurlin's house. We went there often because they were like our kids, but this evening was different. Our Heritage Alliance Church had just started cell groups and Gene had agreed to go. He felt comfortable in their home and enjoyed the people. As the group grew and multiplied into new groups, Gene continued to attend on a fairly regular basis.

On a wintery day early 2002, the cell group was meeting in our living room. The discussion that evening was on heaven and as we were breaking up, Gene's friend, Lloyd, gave him a friendly nudge and said, "I hope I'll be seeing you there." Lloyd left concerned because Gene's answer was non-committal. A couple of weeks later, he made a point of coming to our home and had a personal talk with Gene to be sure where he stood with God. Lloyd was one of the first people to come after Gene's death and he looked me in the eyes and said, "I want you know that Gene is in heaven."

God also gave me a beautiful personal confirmation, because just before I left the Rural Carriers meeting that fateful afternoon, I won a door prize. It was a rustic wood sign with a house on it and the words "Welcome Home."

The moment I received that plaque was about the same time God was welcoming Gene to His heavenly home.

REFERENCES

Cooper, Darien B., *You Can Be the Wife of a Happy Husband*, Shippensburg, PA, Destiny Image Publishers, Inc., 2011

Jones, A. J., *Finding Father, a Journey into the Loving Arms of Daddy God,* Maricopa, AZ, XP Publishing, 2010

Miller, Keith, *A Taste of New Wine,* Bloomington, IN, Author House, 2009

Volkman, Bill, *Basking in His Presence,* Grand Rapids, MI, Dickinson Press, 1996

Warren, Rick, *The Purpose Driven Life,* Grand Rapids, MI, Zondervan, 2012

ACKNOWLEDGMENTS

I am forever grateful to the many people who have shaped my life journey. I am thankful for everyone who believed in and encouraged me to take on this wild adventure of writing a book. My name may be on the front cover but there are many who have helped me get to the finish line.

I want to thank my wonderful children who walked this journey with me. Julie, Linda, David, Rosanne, Karma, Justin, and my grandchildren, Alexis, Emma, Matthew, and Skyler, I could not have done this without you. Rick, Elva, and their children, Kelly and Alex, have been part of my family for thirty years. I want to thank you for letting me take over your dining room when I made it into my writing area. I want to thank the Morris family for their support. I have been "Grammer" to Brett and Shannon's children, Elizabeth, Catherine, Dorothy, Abby, and Jon for thirty years and I have loved being part of their family.

Special thanks to my brother, Pat, and his wife, Elsa, for all their encouragement, support, and prayers. I am so fortunate to have you as my brother.

I want to thank my mother, Aileen Day, who instilled in me at an early age the love of books and writing. She is looking down from heaven with so much pride because of what her daughter has accomplished.

Danny Mullins, you were the first to believe in my story and strongly encouraged me to write this book. Thank you.

I have a wonderful prayer team, and I couldn't have done this without you. Leslie McClure has been my prayer partner for twenty years and is my first go-to person. She has helped with many aspects of this book. It wouldn't be what it is without her. Kay Wolverton, my good friend and travel partner, has always been there for me. Page Geske not only prayed but gave me valuable book advice. Valerie Brechtbill helped with last minute additions, along with her prayers. Thank you, Flora Hill, who prays for me continually. Each person on my prayer team is so special and supportive. Thank you, Joy Kicer, Diane Czekala, Pat Ennis, Sharon Almand, Karen Vanausdeln, Mary Ellen Smith, Shelley Moncrief, Carol Kalbfleisch, Laura O'Connell, and Barb Anderson-Domingues.

In February of 2018, God knew I needed extra encouragement and sent me a special life coach, Chelley Antonczak, who kept me focused on the book.

Thank you, Jane Hoganson, for all the hours you spent proofreading and for the great special suggestions. Thank you, Jan Clodfelder, for your help on picture-taking day.

I want to thank Jonathan Williams for the great cover photo, and my nephew, Bob Keeney, who did the cartoon art of my motor home.

Anna Lebaron, thank you for all your expert knowledge in how to launch my book.

I want to give a special thanks to the late Jim Wies, who gave me so many great ideas before he went to be with the LORD.

This book wouldn't be what it is today if not for my fantastic editor, Zannie Carlson. She took my rough draft and made it into an interesting, entertaining, humorous story. All the little notes and graphics were her brilliant idea. Her skill in editing and formatting made it an easy read and gave my book the character it needed. Zannie, you are a master of words and this book would not exist without your wise, creative, witty, editorial knowledge. I really do appreciate all you have done.

Most of all, I want to acknowledge the Holy Spirit, my God, my Teacher, my Helper, my Comforter, and my Friend. You have continually been with me while writing this book and I thank You for Your constant presence in my life journey. I am thankful that I can partner with You to bring suffering people out of darkness into the Glory light of Jesus. God the Father, Jesus the Son, and Holy Spirit are intertwined as One, and I am so very thankful and eternally grateful for the amazing, everlasting love and grace They shower on me daily.

ABOUT THE AUTHOR

Donna Krueger has truly been a messenger of love and light as she served to bringing others closer to the love of God. She spent most of her life in the Twin Falls, Idaho area where she was active in church, was a Bible study teacher and a jail chaplain, and was an officer and speaker for the Christian Women's Luncheons and Aglow.

Donna is a motivational speaker, personal mentor, and has organized women's retreats. She has served as a Grief/Share facilitator for fourteen years and is currently an Issue Focus Minister with Restoring the Foundations, where she brings hope and healing into shattered lives. She belongs to WIMN (Women in Ministry Network) and is on the intercessor prayer team for Patricia King Ministries.

Donna has savored the joy of being the mother to three children, four grandchildren, and three great-grandchildren. There have been many more who call her mom and grandmother. Donna now lives in Arizona where she is very active with her friends and church family.

Website: www.donnakrueger.com

Email: donnakruegersbook@gmail.com

Facebook: DonnaLKrueger

Instagram: DonnaLKrueger

Made in the USA
Columbia, SC
12 November 2019

83115790R00104